Young Children Learning Through Schemas

Young Children Learning Through Schemas is a creative and highly engaging text that shows how young children can learn through exploring repeated patterns in their actions. With contributions from a range of practitioners, this book examines the philosophical approaches underpinning constructivism and includes a variety of case studies of small children in order to demonstrate the universal explorations we all engage in as human beings.

This approach from the contributors, which involves presenting observations of one or two young children per chapter, is engaging, inspirational and yet rooted in everyday practice. Chapters include a variety of observations of young children at home, in nursery and in groups with their parents or carers, which continue the dialogue about early years practice and the roles of families and professionals. Containing a wealth of illustrative photos, any practitioner researching or working in the area of early years education and care will find this book essential reading.

Cath Arnold is an Early Years Consultant at the Pen Green Research Base in Corby in Northamptonshire.

Katey Mairs worked at the Pen Green Centre since its inception in 1983. She was Deputy Head of the Centre from 1994 until her death in 2008.

Also available in the *Pen Green Books for Early Years Educators* series:

Improving Your Reflective Practice Through Stories of Practitioner Research
Edited by Cath Arnold

Young Children Learning Through Schemas
By Katey Mairs and the Pen Green Team
Edited by Cath Arnold

Developing and Sustaining Children's Centres
By Margy Whalley

Young Children Learning Through Schemas

Deepening the dialogue about learning in the home and in the nursery

Katey Mairs and the
Pen Green Team

Edited by Cath Arnold

Routledge
Taylor & Francis Group

LONDON AND NEW YORK

First published 2013
by Routledge
2 Park Square, Milton Park, Abingdon, Oxon OX14 4RN

Simultaneously published in the USA and Canada
by Routledge
711 Third Avenue, New York, NY 10017

Routledge is an imprint of the Taylor & Francis Group, an informa business

© 2013 Katey Mairs and Cath Arnold

British Library Cataloguing in Publication Data
A catalogue record for this book is available from the British Library

Library of Congress Cataloging in Publication Data
Young children learning through schemas : deepening the dialogue about learning in the home and in the nursery / Edited by Cath Arnold and Katey Mairs.
pages cm. -- (Pen Green books for early years educators)
Includes bibliographical references and index.
ISBN 978-0-415-69731-6 (hardback) -- ISBN 978-0-415-69732-3 (pbk.) -- ISBN 978-0-203-10269-5 (ebook) (print) 1. Schemas (Psychology) in children--Case studies. 2. Emotions in children--Case studies. 3. Cognition in children--Case studies. 4. Mental representation in children--Case studies. I. Arnold, Cath. II. Mairs, Katey, -2008.
BF723.S17Y68 2013
372.21--dc23
2012006222

ISBN: 978-0-415-69731-6 (hbk)
ISBN: 978-0-415-69732-3 (pbk)
ISBN: 978-0-203-10269-5 (ebk)

Typeset in Garamond
by Saxon Graphics Ltd, Derby

MIX
Paper from
responsible sources
FSC
www.fsc.org   FSC® C004839

Printed and bound in Great Britain by the MPG Books Group

Contents

Illustrations

Contributors

Cath Arnold is an Early Childhood Consultant, who has worked in the Early Years Field for 33 years, as a nursery worker, then researcher and writer. Cath has three grown-up children, two quite grown-up grandchildren and a three-year-old grandchild, and has been fascinated by schemas since first hearing of them at Pen Green in 1988.

Chris Athey did various jobs before the Second World War, including farming and toasting teacakes in a sweet factory. She then worked in a factory making teleprinters. She was the only female to work in the tool shop. While working in engineering she became involved in the Workers' Educational Association which led to a year, 1947, at Hillcroft College where she studied philosophy, psychology and literature. This was followed by an Emergency Teacher Training course at Wall Hall Training College. After several years of infant and primary school teaching she ran the Froebel Trainer's Diploma with Joan Tamburrini for most of the 1960s. Following involvement in a pilot study of severely disabled children she was invited to become a Leverhulme Research Fellow at principal lectureship status. This was a post she held for five years (1972–1977) when she directed a Froebel Early Education project. This led to a book published in 1990, called *Extending Thought in Young Children: A Parent Teacher Partnership* (Paul Chapman). A second edition was published in 2007. The 1990 book was the first empirical study of young children that revealed only positive aspects of their thinking. That, and the subsequent edition, have been appreciated by a wide range of professionals and parents and have generated many studies in different countries.

Pam Cubey is a New Zealander, mother of three, grandmother of six, whose 47 years' commitment to early years education was kindled as a young playcentre parent and whose passion with schemas since 1988 owes much to Chris Athey, Tina Bruce and Pen Green, She has been a playcentre educator, professional development facilitator and lecturer, and a researcher for the New Zealand Ministry of Education, including the Centres of Innovation Project.

Annette Cummings is a teacher/senior family worker in the Pen Green nursery and the parent of two children. She originally became involved with the work of the Pen Green Centre as a parent and returned to university in 1996–1997 to gain a PGCE. Annette has undertaken a number of practitioner research projects with staff in the Research Base at Pen Green and has a master's degree in early education with care.

Kate Hayward trained to be a teacher after being involved in the early education of her three children, Tom, Hannah and Emily. Previously she worked in community development projects and health programmes in Britain, Kenya and Papua New Guinea. She is currently a researcher at the Pen Green Research Base, leading on pedagogical support and the professional development programme on parental involvement.

Katey Mairs worked at the Pen Green Centre since its inception in 1983 and sadly died in June 2008 after being unwell for several months. Katey was a real character that we all miss. Her mantra was "Go for it" whenever any of us came up with an idea to try. Katey's love of children shone around all she did and everyone she was with. Katey's kindness, her caring, her sense of humour, together with a very practical approach to life, shaped all of her work and play. Parents knew they could talk with her about their children, their highs and lows, their good days and their bad, and always be listened to; always feel valued and special; never feel judged. She leaves a widower, Ray, and a very special daughter, Ellen, who attended Pen Green Nursery and now teaches in the Early Years locally.

Angela Prodger has worked at Pen Green Centre since 1989: her first day of paid work at the Centre was as a supply worker when staff were all having schema training. She is now the Deputy Head of Centre with overall responsibility for 2–5 years. Angela has one daughter, Ellie, who attended Pen Green Nursery and helped to really bring schemas alive for her.

Colette Tait manages Rushden Community College Children's Centre, a small phase two centre in Northamptonshire. Colette previously worked for many years at Pen Green, where her interest in schemas developed. She has two grown-up children, Georgia and Harry, both of whom attended the Pen Green Nursery.

Margy Whalley was the founding Head of the Pen Green Centre for Under 5s and their families and has worked there since 1983. She has an MA in Community Education and, supported by the Van Leer Foundation and

National Children's Bureau, completed a PhD which focused on Leadership in Integrated Centres. She is currently Director of the Research, Development and Training Base at Pen Green and is involved in research, training and consultancy work both nationally and internationally. On a personal note she has a daughter, Tasha, and is grandmother to Molly and Tom. She is very committed to local politics, loves eating out with friends, visiting new places and meeting new people and is addicted to reading and study.

Foreword

Margy Whalley

> Only an education which takes very seriously the child's view of things can change
> the world for the better
>
> (Janusz Korczak in Bettleheim Recollections and Reflections, p. 195)

Pen Green opened as a community nursery within an integrated centre for children and families in 1983. We were committed from the start to encouraging children to lead their own learning. Katey Mairs, our first passionate and powerful nursery head, who died in 2008, was instrumental in developing our curriculum and pedagogical approach. She knew that rigid structures imposed on children without reference to the context in which they lived and learned were dangerous. At Pen Green we wanted, in Katey's words, for children to feel strong, in control, able to question and able to make good choices. Our concerns were very much about developing children's dispositions to learn and every member of staff who worked with children whether they were NNEB trained or teacher trained, took on the role of family worker engaging with the children and all the important adults in their lives.

In 1983, staff were strongly influenced by Kohl, Holt, Illich and by Sylvia Ashton Warner and Paulo Freire; who both rejected imposed educational systems and structures which fragmented the children's learning experiences and made them dull and irrelevant. It was not until we started working intensively with Chris Athey in 1988, however, that we developed a more conscious and clearly articulated pedagogy which helped us to support and extend children's learning and development (Athey, 1990). Parents who attended that first tea time session on Schemas in the family room at Pen Green in 1988 with Chris Athey, never forgot the experience. They engaged with Chris as equal and active partners committed to supporting their children's learning and development at home and deeply fascinated by the insights that schema theory provided. One parent described how her son was hanging things from trees in the garden, tying ties and string all over the house, connecting up door handles and banisters. 18 years later the same mother talked about the first meeting with Chris Athey and how important her attendance at study groups at Pen Green had been in terms of her developing understanding of her own child's learning. She told me how her son had completed his first year at University, the first child in his family to ever undertake higher education. The parent professional partnership that Chris engendered between family workers and parents at Pen Green was transformational.

Each of the chapters in this book give insights into the ways in which planning for children's learning on the basis of closely observing their schemas leads to a rich and deep experience for the child. Each chapter also shows how sharing knowledge with parents about their children's learning and development in the setting, and learning about the children's development in their homes, results in the development of advocacy and high levels of support for children throughout the education system.

Introduction

Cath Arnold

This book on children's schemas has been with us, as a team, for a long time. The idea of writing a book together was conceptualised at a time when we were meeting regularly with Chris Athey (every six weeks or so) to think about children's development and learning, and to deepen our understanding of schemas. We engaged in day-long sessions and sometimes discussed only three five-minute video sequences during a whole day, which were supported by additional documentation. Sometimes the parents attended and contributed on the day. At other times, we met with families separately. They always made the major contribution. Chris says that she 'never tells people less than they want to know' and she certainly never needed to simplify anything for parents, although there was one memorable occasion when she nearly 'scared the living daylights' out of our 0–3s advisory team, who were invited to join our session for part of the day. (In fairness to them, they are now avid readers of Chris Athey's research and competent trainers in schema theory.) So this book is one outcome of those study days.

Defining what schemas are

The team at Pen Green (several of whom have been working at the centre for more than 20 years) have been studying schemas for at least 24 years. We still find the theory fascinating and we are still figuring out the implications for children and for pedagogy. You will find in this book, that most of the authors attempt to define what schemas are, from Chris Athey's definition in Chapter 1:

> A schema, therefore, can be described as a pattern of repeatable behaviour into which experiences are assimilated and that are gradually co-ordinated. Co-ordinations lead to higher-level and more powerful schemas.

To much simpler explanations:

* a schema is a pattern of repeated actions. Clusters of schemas develop into later concepts (Athey 2003);

- repeated and coherent patterns in play (schemas);
- the 'form' (schema) – what they are 'doing' with what they are playing with.

Each time we articulate our understanding, we become a little clearer about what schemas look like. This book is full of examples of children exploring schemas. It is based on the observations made by workers and parents and the ongoing dialogue between workers and families. We cannot emphasise strongly enough how important those relationships and dialogues are. Sharing schema theory with parents has been significant and has helped them and us understand the children better. Parents know their children well and when we name the patterns, the theory seems to make sense to them right away.

Other theories we have found useful

Many child studies have now been carried out using schematic theory to analyse the data gathered. A strong link many researchers have made is the connection between children's 'involvement' in play and the exploration of schemas (Laevers 1997). Our team almost take for granted that 'involvement' is a prerequisite for 'deep level learning'. For our readers who have not yet come across Ferre Laevers' research on 'involvement' and emotional 'well-being', we would like to briefly introduce both concepts and trust that you will seek out his most recent work.

It was something of a breakthrough for us when we engaged in the Effective Early Learning Project and heard about Laevers' concept of 'involvement' for the first time. Laevers was interested in the processes of learning rather than the outcomes. His focus was on the two 'process variables' of 'involvement' and 'well-being' (Laevers 1997: 15). He describes 'involvement' as

> when children (or adults) are intensely engaged in an activity. They are in a special state. They are concentrating and are eager to continue with the activity. They feel intrinsically motivated to carry on, because the activity falls in with what they want to learn and know i.e. their exploratory drive
>
> (p. 20)

Laevers and his team developed signals and a scale for measuring 'involvement', which is now widely used in Early Childhood settings. Laevers describes 'well-being':

> Children (and adults) who are in a state of well-being, feel like 'fish in water' ... They adopt an open, receptive and flexible attitude towards their environment. A state of well-being results in a fair amount of self-confidence and self-esteem ... They have unhindered contact with their inner selves
>
> (p. 15)

Again, Laevers and his team have developed signals and a scale to monitor well-being.

We have found both concepts extremely useful to share with parents so that we can engage in dialogue using a shared language, including schema theory. You will find the authors of this book referring to these concepts.

The order of the chapters

Chapter 1 is written by Chris Athey and, using her amazing intellectual capacity, she introduces schema theory, drawing on ideas from Plato and Aristotle to Piaget. Chris defines concepts like 'constructivism', 'assimilation' and 'accommodation'. She draws on data from the Froebel Project as examples to illustrate children's schematic play. Chapter 2 is by Annette Cummings and is about Robert, who attended nursery for two years and was very focused on exploring *trajectories*, *enveloping* and *going through a boundary*. Chapter 3 by Cath Arnold is about Caitlin, who also attended the nursery for two years. Part of what fascinated us about Caitlin, was her 'feistiness' and her very strong friendship with Lee. In Chapter 4, Angela Prodger introduces us to Jack, who was very determined to lead his own learning. Chapter 5 was written by Katey Mairs and Cath Arnold. It is about Steffi, who pursued her interest in 'what's inside' over a long period of time. Chapter 6 by Colette Tait introduces us to Ethan and his family, using a drop-in group (Growing Together) and, subsequently, attending the nursery. Colette, together with Ethan's parents, poses some interesting questions about Ethan's *enveloping* schema. In Chapter 7, Kate Hayward offers an account of two children's mark making during their first term at school. One of the children is Caitlin, who we met in Chapter 3. The other is John, who was very focused on ladders, H's, and noughts and crosses (all *grid*-like shapes). Chapter 8 is a little different. It is written by Pam Cubey, a colleague from New Zealand. Pam has introduced schema theory to some settings in New Zealand and the parents in those settings have become very involved in observing their own children and sharing their learning about schematic play. Pam tells us a little of the Playcentre Movement and brings together Learning Stories and schemas, which she convincingly views as complementary. Included in the chapter are three short case studies of children from their parents' perspectives. Chapter 9 by Cath Arnold draws together some of the ideas from the book and addresses some common queries about schemas.

Chapter 1

Beginning with the theory about schemas

Chris Athey

This chapter introduces the theory:

* thinking about inner and outer factors involved in learning
* assimilation
* some common schemas and the ways they are explored
* the difference between 'content' and 'form'
* some examples from the Froebel Project
* co-ordinations, and
* major accommodations.

Inner and outer factors

Learning, from birth, is typically discussed under two main headings and has been since Plato and Aristotle.

First is the part that children contribute to their own learning. These are inner factors. Second are the aspects of the world that children learn about. These are external factors. There is, understandably, a great emphasis on children learning about aspects of the world that adults approve of. Most adults place great emphasis on agreeable social behaviours as opposed to behaviour considered to be antisocial. Good behaviour is easier to live with.

Professionals in education talk about the mathematical aspects of the world, the physical aspects, the language aspects and so on. Recently these aspects of the curriculum have been discussed under 'domains' of learning. Elizabeth Carruthers and Maulfry Worthington have produced an important book showing how schemas develop into conventional mathematical concepts (Worthington and Carruthers 2003). Molly Davies started with schemas and showed how these develop into conventional forms of movement and dance (Davies 2003).

In recent times, adults involved in education and schooling have not necessarily been experts in education. Under the heading of 'inclusiveness', a much wider range of adults than hitherto are now concerned with upbringing, care and education.

Children's contributions to their own learning are psychological and this is what is mainly discussed in this book. The authors of this book discuss psychological structures (or schemas) and psychological processes. Processes are the means by which the learner moves from early to later, more complex, learning.

As a simplification it could be said that all learning has its inner and outer aspects. Recently there have been attempts to recategorise some outer features of the world which have been used as 'jogs' to memory (aides memoires) such as the contents of a Filofax, as 'memory' itself. The arguments are interesting and clever but will not be discussed here, partly because many of the arguments are simply word play but mainly because of lack of space.

The aspects of learning that focus on things 'out there' in the world are usually referred to as 'learning by experience'.

There is no doubt that children do learn by experience but the term 'experiencing' needs to be clarified. There is more to it than the learner simply being confronted by something in the world and thereby experiencing it. Real experiencing always requires the cognitive or thinking participation of the learner either consciously or non-consciously. John Dewey (1938 [1976]) said that information had to be psychologised before it could be called knowledge.

In the United Kingdom, probably because of our philosophical background and other factors, more importance is given to the erroneous idea that children learn directly from experience than to ways in which children construct their own knowledge.

Assimilation

Piaget described 'experiencing' as assimilation to schemas as follows:

> Children do not just learn directly from aspects of environment. They learn by assimilating material, ideas and situations in the world into inner schemas and concepts.
>
> (Piaget 1953: 384)

Schemas transform the raw data of experience into meaningful and manageable units. Raw data is too messy and voluminous for the brain to deal with efficiently. Schemas sort out a large amount of data into fewer categories. These categories, like later concepts, are easier to manage than trying to hold on to a heap of content.

Most people know that when they take a particular interest in something, or somebody, the world suddenly seems full of stuff, unnoticed before, relevant to the new interest. Presumably that stuff has been in the external world all along but unnoticed because of its lack of particular significance. Schemas give content of a certain kind particular significance at particular times.

Schemas and concepts are *forms* of understanding brought to bear on disparate bits and pieces of the world. As Hunt, in his illuminating book called *Intelligence and Experience* (1961: 279), puts it: 'At each age and level the environmental circumstances must supply encounters for the child which permit him to use the repertoire of schemas that he has already developed'. Experience is always assimilated to cognitive structures and this is how knowledge is acquired. Increase experiences and schemas (or forms of thought) will be enriched. A schema, therefore, can be described as a pattern of repeatable behaviour into which experiences are assimilated and that are gradually co-ordinated. Co-ordinations lead to higher-level and more powerful schemas.

Forms of thought up to the age of about five or six are usually called schemas and from six onwards they are called concepts. This is a convention that started with Immanuel Kant (1781/1787 [1963]) who wrote about the route from schematism to systems. In Piaget's book *Structuralism*, he discusses the route from schemas, which become increasingly co-ordinated until they become systems of concepts. He does not, however, illustrate this developmental route with real-life examples from children. This is what an increasingly large number of professionals are trying to do now and this is what this book is about.

The main finding about attempts to extend schemas in various situations is that schemas are generalisable to many different populations. They are probably universal. Staff of Pen Green have been working closely with professionals in the UK, Australia, New Zealand, China, Portugal and Germany, and in all of those countries parents, workers and researchers have observed similar patterns of action and representation (schemas).

At the core of 'hard' science is invariance of meaning. This means that everybody must agree on the rules or laws central to that particular domain. As soon as some kind of uncertainty of meaning creeps in everybody concerned jumps to attention and one of two things happen:

- The research that has challenged the invariant law is smartly dispatched as flawed or unreliable.
- Alternatively, the law is changed so that it accommodates to the challenge.

There are no loose ends. In traditional 'hard' science everybody must agree. There is no such agreement in the social sciences. The term 'schema' is used in a multitude of ways, most of which have no relevance to working with young children.

Since the publication of Athey's book *Extending Thought in Young Children* in 1990, many people in different countries have adopted schematic learning theory as an important aspect of an extremely useful theory of education.

Most 'progressive' teachers are already 'constructivists' in that they are 'child-centred'. The term 'schemas' has been long used with infants but not with children from two to five. After age five, the term 'concepts' is usually adopted. In 1990, schema theory within constructivism was seriously undeveloped in relation to children between two and five. These years were the dark ages of child development. Most of the following definitions by professionals who are developing 'schemas' and the broader theory of 'constructivism' help to 'flesh out' the definitions given by Athey in 1990. The original definitions from *Extending Thought* were taken from classical sources such as Kant and Piaget and applied to the empirical findings of the Froebel Project.

Tina Bruce, who worked in the Froebel Project, helped to expand on the meaning of schemas. She states:

> Children's schemas seem to make children alert to certain events and properties of objects in their environment. Schemas seem to be part of their motivation for learning, their insatiable drive to move, represent, discuss, question and find out. Children seem to take from the environment the elements that make sense to them and that match their schemas at the time.
>
> (quoted in van Wijk *et al.* 2006: 14)

(Most of the authors of the Wilton Playcentre book have worked very closely with the Pen Green authors of this book. They are Nikolien van Wijk, Ainsley Simmonds, Pam Cubey, Linda Mitchell and others.)

Anne Meade, a New Zealand researcher and advisor to the Wilton experiment, is quoted in *Transforming Learning at Wilton Playcentre'*. She sees schemas as:

> pieces of thought ... not like the pieces of a jigsaw, because they don't fit in only one place. Perhaps the best metaphor is that schemas are like pieces of Lego which can be fitted into lots of different structures, in this instance, the structures [are] cognitive structures.
>
> (Meade 1995: 2)

Common schemas

Examples of common schemas illustrated in the chapters of this book include the following.

Trajectories are the most basic schemas identified in the Froebel Project. Trajectories refer to all forms of movement taking place in all directions.

Containing, enclosing and enveloping are ubiquitous schemas. By age four most boys have discarded the handbag in favour of the postman's sack or the doctor's bag. There are social constraints on 'content'. Handbags are classified as women's stuff. Half a century ago a container might have been represented as a bag of coal. Now it is more likely to be a bag carrying a laptop. Historical and social changes affect 'content' but containing and enveloping are invariant over time and space.

Rotation reflects an interest in all things that turn: wheels, taps, rolling, twirling one's own body. When schemas are co-ordinated, thought becomes more powerful in that more complex schematic relationships can absorb and transform more content.

When children's schematic actions, rather than content, are observed, children's approaches to learning can be interpreted differently. It is through schemas and the fitting of content to different schematic threads that children's own constructions of reality and subsequent continuity can be identified. Looking at learning in this way can be a little like unlocking a door, shining a light on previously darkened areas, seeing anew (Nutbrown 1994: 36).

Schemas explored in different ways

Athey (1990) showed that these schemas manifest themselves in different ways:

1   An early way of exploring patterns is through actions. We call these 'sensory-motor' explorations.
2   When something is used to stand for something else, children begin to use 'symbolic representation'. Symbolic representations use actions, mark making and other graphic forms and speech.
3   Functional Dependency Relationships are based on actions with their effects: 'If I throw this ball harder than before, it will go further'. 'Do this sort of thing, then that will happen'. Literature in English on this stage of development is sparse. It became necessary during the Froebel Project to have a book by Piaget and colleagues, published in French, translated into English. British researchers often erroneously call these relationships 'cause and effect'. Someone is needed to study these relationships. A working knowledge of French would be an advantage.
4   'Thought'. There are many different definitions of 'thought', most of which are not suitable for the study of young children. An 'operational' definition of 'thought' was adopted during the Froebel Project. 'Thought' was being manifested when children were able to recall and represent events about people and objects without needing concrete reminders of the original experience.

The above four ways of functioning may be seen as a progression in 'coming to know'. However, we do not leave these earlier ways of knowing and understanding behind. Schemas gradually increase in complexity and we continue to draw on all of these ways of finding out and understanding throughout our lives.

Although there were relatively few instances of abstract thought noted during the Froebel Project they were all interesting because, in relation to every child, observations showing evidence of children's thinking consisted of clear internalisations of earlier schematic concerns.

Careful observation can lead to a greater understanding of progression from Action to Thought becoming more visible and better documented. Professional concepts are cumulative and planning for further learning becomes easier over time.

Content and form

When considering children's schemas, Athey makes an important distinction between 'form' and 'content'. A schema is a cognitive structure, a spontaneous 'form' of thought. Content refers to something specific in the environment. Things in the environment remain 'as they are'. Frogs remain frogs and windmills remain windmills until they are assimilated into the mind. This is when those things acquire cognitive 'form'. An important role of the teacher is to feed spontaneous structures ['form'] with a wide array of 'content' (Athey 1990: 41). When the Froebel Project adults helped to extend the range of objects that shared a common property, by naming, they were fleshing out 'form' [schemas] by extending 'content'.

Nutbrown provides examples of how 'forms' of thought (schemas) once identified can be nourished with worthwhile 'content'. For example, if a child is focusing on a particular schema related to roundness we would say that child is working on a circular schema. The form is 'roundness' and the content can be anything that extends this form: wheels, rotating machinery, rolling a ball, the spinning of planets and so on (Nutbrown 1994: 1). Infants are born with a repertoire of schemas which are biologically predetermined and which, as they mature, integrate and transform into ever more complex and sophisticated forms. The socio-cultural aspects of schemas are to do with the way that experience, as opposed to biological maturation, influences the development of schemas throughout childhood and also through our adult lives. Because the two are in a perpetual state of interaction, each influences the other causing changes, modifications and transformations (Bruce 1997: 68).

Focusing on the 'content' at the expense of 'form' can lead to the conclusion that young children 'flit' from one theme [or content] to another and that they are unsystematic (Bruce 1997: 83).

We may describe them as 'flitters' but they may be 'fitters', fitting various kinds of content into one schema. Meade has said that rather than thinking of them as butterflies we could see them as honeybees moving from flower to flower, gathering nectar to build something of value (Meade and Cubey 1995: 18).

Meade and Cubey found that teachers often needed more content knowledge themselves in order to be able to help children move to 'higher levels of intellectual development involving abstract thought'. 'At higher levels of schema development this has to involve discussion' [between child and adult] (1995: 68).

There is less difficulty in identifying schemas than there is in extending them. The most difficult of all is to start with very early schemas and to trace continuities to later aspects of the curriculum.

The kind of research methodology that all of the authors of this book and the researchers just mentioned, including researchers in Beijing, share, is best described as 'illuminative research and evaluation'. This method involves making close and detailed observations of children pursuing self-chosen activities. Simultaneous with this close observation is the search for continuing illumination on the fundamental meaning of what it is that is being observed. A search for meaning must be carried out within an explanatory theory.

Examples from the Froebel Project

Schemas lie beneath the surface of manifest behaviour. The examples I am going to give now are from the early days in our Froebel Project.

Alistair pretended to be a captain of a ship. He kept diving into the water to rescue his sailors. I think at the time I described that as: 'Al is pretending to be a captain'. I did not focus on the 'trajectory' aspect of the pretence. Provision was more to do with captains and ships (caps and life belts) than questions about the starting point of the dive or the end point of the rescue. Later, I observed that Alistair was preparing to go on a picnic. Picnics bring out the worst in teachers. Their managerial side takes over and there are complaints based on the closely observed rule that 'everything has a place and there is a place for everything'. This leads to disgruntled teachers saying: 'How many times have I told you not to take those things out of the home area?'

Later still, Al's pretence is about a bus that crashes and the wounded are carried off to hospital. If we look at the rescue, the picnic and the bus crash in terms of content then we can say that the three situations are quite different and we will have to make three different kinds of provision. This is exhausting and all teachers know when the 'moment' has passed. However, careful and informed reflection based on professional knowledge of schemas, reveal what the three situations have in common. They are all to do with trajectories with starting and end points. In these three cases, straight line trajectories are the common and shared structures of action and cognition that lie under the manifold and various surface content of what children are representing. Recognising and extending schemas, or forms of thought, helps teachers to give developmentally appropriate help without the exhaustion of trying to develop themes based on different content.

From a broader point of view, the world would be a different and better place today if education concentrated more on what all human beings share instead of focusing on differences or making comparisons.

These days people give 'mission statements' which are banner headlines behind aims and objectives. Perhaps mission statements help to draw attention to fundamental values. All educational endeavour starts with values. We want to produce people who have the sort of characteristics we admire and would like to see more of. I heard Mary-Jane Drummond say she would like children to think for themselves and feel for others. I thought this was very good as a mission statement. I imagine that most readers of this book might agree with that. However, there are people in power who do not want children to think for themselves. People who think for themselves are more difficult to manage.

If one of the aims of early education is to help develop quality of mind in children then we must try to find out more about 'mind'. There are now thousands of neuroscientists trying to find out more about 'brain 'and some about 'brain' and 'mind'. It is likely that some of the unsolved, ongoing, problems that have been around for hundreds of years will be solved or, at least taken forward with the help of new kinds of technology.

Until the 1970s there was a mainline theory around about young children's minds. The theory was both unattractive and untrue and of no use to parents or teachers. This theory maintained that children between the ages of two and six were mentally inadequate. It was said that they couldn't concentrate on anything for very long, they shifted from one interest to another. This was called 'flitting'.

The example I have just given of Alistair pretending to be a captain, a picnicker and then a bus driver would be an example of 'flitting'.

It is true that children do shift from content to content. However, people aware of schemas would call this 'fitting', rather than 'flitting'. Alistair is fitting three different kinds of content into a form of thought to do with trajectories. The more content children can fit into their schemas the better, on the grounds that well-nourished schemas are better than poverty-stricken schemas.

Other aspects of a deficit theory which is still being peddled in many institutes of education is that young children cannot conserve number, their spatial concepts are all over the place, they cannot classify, they cannot put things into order and this is the worst, they cannot even perform one-to-one correspondence.

I like an anecdote I read once that every time Albert Einstein met Piaget he would say, 'I say, Jean, tell me that funny story again about young children not being able to conserve.'

In short, before 1970 young children were mainly described in terms of what they could *not* do. The general description of this dire state of affairs was that children from two to five were 'pre-operational'. One could well understand politicians deciding to put off paying for real education until children were old enough to benefit from it.

All theories, even bad ones, require some kind of supporting empirical evidence. However, even hard empirical evidence can give rise to different interpretations depending on the values and the knowledge of the person doing the interpreting.

These days there are many more attractive theories around regarding the cognitive abilities of young children. The one I particularly like is that young children resemble scientists in the way they think. Alison Gopnik and her colleagues wrote a book called *The Scientist in the Crib* (1999). These researchers from Harvard take a constructivist view of development. They believe that children contribute to their own learning and are busy trying to find out how.

They ask similar questions to the sort that are being asked by researchers at Pen Green and other constructivist researchers. Some very important questions are on the *processes* of learning. How do children get from an early stage of thinking and learning to a later and more complex stage of thinking and learning? For half a century there has been evidence showing wide differences between child and adult thinking but there is very little on more minute increments of cognitive advance. There is a large amount of research from America on 'metaphor' but nothing linking 'schemas' with 'metaphor' in spite of the obvious links between motor action and later metaphor.

The Gopnik researchers ask useful questions about developmental advances but their research methodology rather cuts across the search for processes that take thinking forward from early to later stages. They use many research studies to map-out broad stages of development in the early years. This is a bit like building up a jigsaw. However, an external map does not necessarily lend itself to the identification of the minute processes of development in individuals. However, the book is very useful in many ways, particularly for a range of games that adults can play with infants of different ages and stages. The games are definitely 'developmentally appropriate' because they are linked with specific research findings.

I agree with Gopnik that the thinking of young children does resemble the thinking of scientists, not in generalised ways as put forward by Gopnik and colleagues, but in highly specific ways.

Examples of very early thinking in infants from the work of Tom Bower put next to high level thinking of geniuses from Capra suggest that similarities between infants and scientists lie in the process of making co-ordinations of schemas or concepts.

Co-ordinating schemas

Tom Bower showed that infants in the first month track objects which move between points, such as the family cat. Infants also gaze at points of departure and points of arrival. In other words, infants have two main strategies for understanding the world, 'gazing' and 'tracking'. Like all schemas, these behaviours are repeated and applied to a lot of different situations (Piaget

1951 [1962]: 274). Repeated schemas lead to generalisations and these generalisations develop into early categories and then into logical classifications. To spell this out: very early on infants come to the conclusion that some things move and some things do not. And, of course, that is quite right as far as it goes.

Gazing leads to knowledge of the configuration or the shape and details of objects. Tracking leads to knowledge of the movement aspects of objects, including self and other persons.

This next point is very important as far as the process of co-ordination is concerned. Initially, gazing and tracking are two separate forms of behaviour. We know this because if an experimenter makes a stationary object move, a very young infant will continue to gaze at the blank space. Similarly, if a moving object is stopped, the infant will continue to track. One of the first great accommodations and co-ordinations take place when infants realise that some objects are stationary and some objects move but some objects can be stationary *or* move (Bower 1974, 1977). This realisation, like all accommodations and co-ordinations, transforms objects in the world in that everything is seen in a new light.

I think what links the thinking of young children with the complexities of later thinking is the mechanism and the consequences of making new co-ordinations between previously separate aspects of knowing.

Some of these are dramatic and give rise to exclamations such as 'Oh, yes!' 'Eureka!' 'Of course', 'The penny dropped!' 'I suddenly saw the light!' 'I put two and two together!' Less dramatically, during learning we could say that what is 'known' leads to what becomes 'better known' and so on. Such co-ordinations have an agreeable affective or emotional component. The more we know the more we want to know.

Increasing understanding of early earning might be by first 'spotting schemas', then extending with worthwhile content and then trying to document the co-ordination of schemas which lead to higher order co-ordinations which are then called 'concepts'.

The co-ordination of concepts is a process that takes place during the cognitive development of individuals. At a very, very, very high level there are people such as Newton who make such high level co-ordinations from concepts that are already known so that human knowledge itself takes a giant step forward.

Capra's book *The Turning Point* traces the development of public knowledge and he documents how each stage of knowledge is firmly grounded in what has gone before:

> Newton brought about a grand synthesis of the concepts of Copernicus, Kepler, Bacon, Galileo and Descartes. By doing so he brought about the crowning achievement of seventeenth century science. By pure thought he combined the most advanced concepts of the day and thereby

formulated a new method of mathematics known as differential calculus. The new thinking was firmly grounded in the thinking that was already there although shared with very few people. For the first time in history here was a theory that could describe the motion of solid bodies (think of apples) being pulled towards the ground and planets being pulled towards the sun. He used his new mathematical method to formulate the exact laws of motion for all bodies under the influence of the force of gravity.

(Capra 1982: 49)

Newton was a genius in that he was able to combine so many advanced concepts into a new synthesis.

Some of the latest research on the brain show that new co-ordinations are not necessarily triggered by external situations. In fact most new co-ordinations take place between one set of brain cells and another. You suddenly 'see the light' as one cell assembly connects up with another. However, any new syntheses of thought in any one of us, from birth onwards, brings new illumination to things we already know at some level. Knowledge increasingly transforms the world and makes everything more interesting. This is one of the real purposes of education: to facilitate excitements of the mind.

What makes the blinding insights of every infant in the world different from the blinding insights of a Darwin or a Newton is that individual co-ordinations of knowledge illuminate individual understandings but geniuses make new co-ordinations that are world-shaking in that they add to the history of human knowledge.

One of the useful aspects of the theory that knowledge is built up from previous co-ordinations is that it shifts our judgement from absolute terms such as 'right' and 'wrong' to an alternative view that all knowledge is partial. This is not to say that there is no such thing as inaccurate knowledge but that looking at knowledge as incomplete or partial is more useful as a research tool than judgements based on absolute notions of 'right' and 'wrong'.

There are many themes in this book that might help professionals in the Early Years of education to sharpen their professional concepts.

- There is 'cognitive structure': 'schemas and concepts'.
- There are the processes of learning: 'assimilation and accommodation'.
- There is the whole issue of how children make connections between schemas.
- There is the under-researched issue of psychological 'continuity' and 'development' between early and later learning.

Each theme when studied, and co-ordinated with the others will help build a 'constructivist' pedagogy for the early years.

Reflections and questions

- What do I mean by a 'constructivist pedagogy'?
- How do we think about knowledge? Do we think of it as a body of facts or concepts waiting to be discovered? Or do we think of knowledge as internal, to do with 'knowing'?
- Can you think of examples of schemas being co-ordinated?
- When I talk about 'facilitating excitements of the mind' to what am I referring?

Chapter 2

A case study about Robert

Annette Cummings

Introduction

This chapter is about a child called Robert who came to Pen Green Nursery, in September 2000, aged two years and five months. This chapter sets out to:

- document some of Robert's early explorations at Nursery using the shaving foam and at the woodwork bench;
- document Robert's parents' observations in a portfolio; and
- give an account of Robert talking to a group of six Early Childhood Specialists, including Chris Athey, about his current interests and concerns and reflecting on his earlier learning, at age six.

Throughout this chapter I hope to highlight a strong link between Robert's early schematic play and his later emergent mathematical thinking.

Robert's home context

> Schemas are both biologically pre-determined and socio-culturally influenced and so they change and modify according to who children meet and grow up with, where and when.
>
> (Bruce 1997: 73).

Robert's parents, Susan and Chris, have supported Robert through his time at Nursery and they continue to support him at school. When Robert was in Nursery, from September 2000 to July 2002, Susan was actively engaged at the centre. She attended the Parents Involvement in their Children's Learning study group (PICL) on a weekly basis and kept a diary of Robert's key concerns and interests at home. Susan was also elected as a parent representative on the centre's policy board and has spoken at two national conferences held at Pen Green, on documenting children's learning (October 2002 and October 2004).

Chris has two hobbies, cricket and painting miniature war-game figures, which have had a strong influence on Robert's family home life. The family often spend weekends away visiting war-gaming events where battles are re-enacted in miniature. Chris also plays cricket for the Stewarts and Lloyds Corby team. Susan, Jennifer (Robert's older sister) and Robert are all involved in both hobbies.

Robert at Nursery: September 2000 – July 2002

Robert joined my family group for his second year at nursery. Through close observation of Robert at Nursery and building up good relationships with his parents I was able to plan individual worthwhile provision to meet Robert's interests and cognitive concerns.

Robert displayed a cluster of complementary schemas in his play at Nursery:

* Trajectory – moving in or creating lines in space.
* Envelopment or covering over. Envelopment is where children envelop, cover over or surround self or objects in some way.
* Going through a boundary – 'causing oneself or material or an object to go through a boundary and emerge at the other side' (Arnold 1999: 22).

Trajectory example

Narrative observation

Robert (two years and seven months) settled outside in the Discovery Area when he came to Nursery today. The hose was attached to the tap and Robert ran to the welly rack and put a pair of wellies on. He then asked the adult to help him with his waterproof jacket.

Holding the hose, Robert walked toward a small chair in the area and directed the force of the water on the back of the chair (Figure 2.1). The back of the chair had slats in it and some of the water escaped. As Robert moved closer to the chair he was able to aim the water directly at the wooden slats. Robert then walked in front of the chair and aimed the hose. The force of the water knocked the chair over and Robert was very pleased with himself. He quickly returned to his original position, behind the chair. Robert kept the hose in this position for five minutes. He then raised the hose in the act of displacing water and wetting himself all over!

Analysis and discussion

Robert (two years and ten months) was developing an understanding of the concept of pressure and force. The closer he grew towards the chair, the pressure of the water increased, knocking the chair over. By directing the hose into the air Robert was exploring how high the water would go. Robert was confident to go off and explore the other resources in the Nursery.

Figure 2.1 Robert and the hose.

Envelopment example

Narrative observation

Robert (two years and eight months) came into Nursery and headed towards his special box. He took out a small box of face paints and walked towards the Block Area. A face painting table had already been set up in the Nursery and Robert sat down and waited until it was time to have his turn. When his turn eventually arrived he pointed to a picture in the face painting book of a green monster. Robert sat very still while his face was painted. Once finished, Robert looked closely at his face and began to smudge the black circles on his face (Figure 2.2). Robert enjoyed covering his face with paint when he came to Nursery. This was a common pattern of behaviour for Robert. The face paint seemed to give him confidence to go off and explore the other resources in the Nursery. Robert had his own set of face paints in his special box.

Figure 2.2 Robert and the face paints.

Analysis and discussion

Robert was learning about covering an area of his body, his face. Bruce (1997: 79) believes that early envelopment schema can lead to the later concept of 'area in mathematics'.

Going through a boundary example

Narrative observation

Robert (aged two years and six months) was very interested in the garlic press. At first he needed some help to place the dough inside the small compartment and squeeze the dough out of the other side. Through practice, Robert could manage this activity unaided after a short time (Figure 2.3). Once the dough had come out Robert squashed it up and place it back in the compartment ready to repeat the process. Robert had to concentrate very hard and press the handles together with all of his strength. Robert stayed with this activity for 15 minutes.

Analysis and discussion

Robert was learning about the amount of force he had to apply on the handles of the garlic press to make the dough come out of the other end like 'worms'. He was also learning about the mathematical concepts of wholes, parts and division, by dividing the dough into 'worms' and squashing it back into one whole 'lump'.

Figure 2.3 Robert using the garlic press.

The importance of observation

Identifying and supporting children's schemas are essential if children are to understand or make sense of their world. Robert, like all nursery children, was closely observed by all nursery staff. Researching through Robert's Celebration of Achievement file I was able to identify 52 incidents of Robert using his Trajectory schema, 56 Going Through and 41 incidents of his Envelopment schema. Generally when children are playing schematically they are intrinsically motivated to learn, resulting in long periods of concentration. Through their schemas, children are 'fitting' various experiences into their current thinking. 'Clusters of schemas develop into later higher order concepts' (Athey 2003). Robert's cluster of schemas, combined with the family interests, have given Robert a starting point to explore his mathematical ideas.

> Good early years education leads to high level concept formation
>
> (Athey 2004)

Some examples of early observations of Robert at Nursery and home

Here are some examples of Robert using his Trajectory, Envelopment and Going Through schemas at Nursery and at home.

Trajectory and lines

Age	Activity
2.4.8	Running from point to point in the Nursery
2.5.5	Building towers in the Block area and taking them down again (trajectory line)
2.5.14	Watching a diving competition on the TV at home and jumping off the sofa
3.0.0	Using a beater to make louder sounds with the African drum
3.2.0	Coming down the slide repeatedly
3.4.22	Beating piano keys and singing
3.7.4	Watching Santa abseil from a roof climbing trees and jumping
3.7.11	Making worms longer by pulling both ends
3.10.3	Lifting the gates in the water feature to make the water gush down
3.10.14	Using a stick as a microphone, singing 'Reach for the Stars'

Envelopment

Age	Activity
2.5.5	Going in a green barrel and covered-squeals of delight
2.6.7	Covering toast with cheese and immersing it in water
2.6.19	Enveloping his hands with cornflour
3.0.0	Had his hands and face painted
3.1.0	At sink wearing hat and rucksack
3.5.10	Covering hands and head with wet sand
3.7.4	Enveloping computer screen with colour
3.8.12	Washing self with bubbles at the sink
3.10.3	Jumping in and out of puddles to get muddy
3.10.8	Wearing a Dalmatian outfit/building a den
3.11.2	Wearing a mask
4.0.1	Enveloping hands and face in paint
4.1.2	Washing bathroom walls and mirror
4.3.4	Placing a dinosaur inside a rubber glove and filling it with water – 'It's big but it's little'

Going through a boundary

Age	Activity
2.4.27	Blowing through a straw
2.6.7	Connecting an electric circuit
2.6.14	Pushing trains through tunnels
3.0.0	Choosing a difficult route-going through tyres to reach the platform
3.2.0	Blowing through tubing to create bubbles/experimenting with garlic press to push dough through
3.4.22	Pouring sand through a funnel and into a tube
3.8.12	Wearing earphones to listen and respond
3.9.0	Playing the birdsong whistle all afternoon 'This is my best noise'
3.10.8	Using the sand timers
3.11.2	Using tubing to project his voice

Co-ordinations of Robert's schemas

Here are four detailed observations in which Robert co-ordinated his trajectory, envelopment and going through a boundary schemas.

Robert and the shaving foam

I videoed Robert (four years) using the shaving foam for over one and a half hours (Figure 2.4). Throughout that period he had intense periods of exploration, concentration and mastery. I then edited the video to make a short film of six and a half minutes called *Robert and the Shaving Foam* (April 2000).

Robert was struggling with the nozzle of the can. The worker intervened when Robert needed some help, suggesting, 'Why don't you put your thumbs on there?' Robert could not manage to press the nozzle with enough force. She then suggested that he used 'two fingers'. Robert clearly understood this suggestion but used four fingers to depress the button. The shaving foam appeared. Robert squirted large amounts of the shaving foam onto his hands and then made circular movements on his cheeks (envelopment).

Robert applied the shaving foam to envelop the back of his neck, under his chin and onto his hair. Squirting out more foam he tilted his chin up and closed his eyes and mouth and began to gently massage these areas.

Robert continued to envelop his hands, mouth, cheeks, ears, forehead, hair and jumper with the shaving foam. He repeatedly applied the foam to these areas and persevered in this exploration for 25 minutes. Robert was 'deeply

Figure 2.4 Robert and the shaving foam.

involved' in this self-initiated play (Laevers 1997: 18–19). Eventually the shaving foam began to run out and only squirts of foam appeared. He looked very closely at the trajectory of the foam and watched as it fell to the ground. As he continued to depress the nozzle, air came out of the can, making gurgling noises. Robert found this episode very funny and began to dance with joy.

We could see Robert's delight after looking at himself in the mirror and he mentioned to me that he was 'having a shave like my dad'. One of the general characteristics of learning based on children's schematic or cognitive concerns are their expressions of deep satisfaction. These are what the staff at Pen Green call being 'chuffed' (Tait 2004).

ANALYSIS AND DISCUSSION

What were the early concepts that Robert was exploring?

- Area – he was finding out the area he could cover with a handful of shaving foam.
- Weight – full/empty, the can eventually ran out of foam.
- Force – the amount of force he needed to put on the nozzle to make it work.
- Air pressure – Robert could hear the air coming out of the can as it gurgled and could see the shaving foam expand on his hand.

Children explore and express schemas in different ways:

- Through their senses and actions
  Robert was enjoying the feeling and smell of the shaving foam as he smoothed it over his face with a circular hand motion.
- Symbolically – making something stand for something else.
  Robert was exploring his envelopment schema at a symbolically when he was pretending to have a shave, like his dad.
- Through functional dependency – if I do this, then, as a consequence, that will happen.
  Robert discovered that the emergence of shaving foam is functionally dependent on the force of his action of pressing the nozzle.
- Through their thoughts – This is where children convey the meaning in the absence of any perceptual reminder of the actual event (the experience has been internalised).
  Robert told his mum about having a shave at Nursery.

Through his schematic play Robert was autonomous, displaying persistence, determination and mastery. He was developing a strong disposition to learn (Dweck and Leggett (1988), *Te Whäriki* (1993)).

Robert and the woodwork bench

> Through observations of children's schemas we can see the early development of mathematical concepts.
>
> (Worthington and Carruthers 2003: 38)

There is evidence to demonstrate that Robert combined his schemas – Trajectory, Going Through and Envelopment when he worked at the woodwork bench. The woodwork bench was one of Robert's favourite places in the nursery. He was often found deeply engaged in this type of activity where his levels of involvement were very high (Laevers 1997). Over time, Robert became a very skilled woodworker. I have observations of Robert using the woodwork bench throughout his time at nursery. He was competent at using different types of saws to cut wood and using a hammer and nails to construct different models. More often than not Robert chose to wear goggles or an apron when engaged in this type of play.

NARRATIVE OBSERVATION

When Robert (three years and one month) came to Nursery he stopped at the woodwork bench and noticed a large piece of hardwood. As the paint pots were nearby he helped himself to some blue paint and enveloped the wood in paint. He then left the area. Later, Robert returned to the woodwork bench. He was wearing an apron and a pair of goggles (envelopment). He found his blue piece of wood and secured it in the vice the correct way. Robert then picked up the large saw in one hand and attempted to saw the wood along its length.

The adult in the area demonstrated to Robert the correct way to hold the saw and cut through the wood (Figure 2.5). Robert persisted in this activity and realised that he had to work very hard to cut through the wood (trajectory and going through). After a short time Robert stopped sawing and noticed the sawdust on the floor. He placed the saw back in the same groove and continued with his task. Eventually Robert succeeded in his self-chosen activity and cut through the wood. He was very pleased with himself.

ANALYSIS AND DISCUSSION

Robert may be beginning to explore the following concepts:

- Division – by cutting the length of wood into pieces.
- Subtraction – each time Robert cuts off a piece of wood, his original piece gets shorter.
- Force – the amount of force he uses on the saw depends how quickly he can cut through the wood.

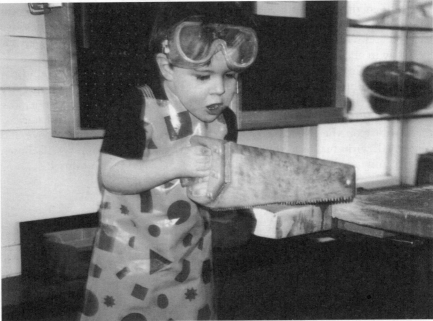

Figure 2.5 Robert and the woodwork bench.

Robert and the hammer

NARRATIVE OBSERVATION

Robert (three years and three months) came to the woodwork bench and picked up a claw hammer. He noticed some long nails and picked them up. Robert now had the claw hammer in his right hand and the nails in his left. He then placed them down on the bench and found himself a small piece of wood. Robert then picked up one of the nails and held it in his hand over the wood. Picking up the hammer he gently tapped the nail on the head to secure it in place. Robert then placed the hammer down and tested out the nail to make sure it was secure, ready for hammering. He then lifted up the hammer with two hands and banged the nail firmly into the wood (Figure 2.6).

ANALYSIS AND DISCUSSION

Robert realised that the claw hammer was very heavy to lift with one hand. He demonstrated that he needed to secure the nail in the wood before hammering it and that by using two hands on the hammer the nail would be firmly fixed into the wood. By these actions, Robert was exploring an early understanding of the concepts of weight and force. He understood that the amount of force he used on the hammer determined how quickly the nail was driven into the wood. Both of these actions were functionally dependent on Robert actions.

Figure 2.6 Robert hammering nails into wood.

By the time Robert was ready to move onto 'big school' he had experienced two years of a stimulating and rich environment at nursery and four years at home. His mathematical development had been nurtured and extended through his schemas and he was cognitively challenged to broaden his mathematical thinking.

Robert and the rubber gloves

NARRATIVE OBSERVATION

Robert (four years, three months and two days) and his friend, Owen, came running outside carrying rubber gloves. Robert stopped at the Discovery Area and filled his glove with water. He then let Owen fill his glove with water. Both the boys then ran outside and threw them on the ground with a splat and laughed at each other. They then picked the gloves up and ran to the tap refilling the gloves. As the water filled the fingers of the gloves Robert and Owen laughed as the weight of the water elongated the glove fingers. They then ran outside and threw them on the ground. Robert then picked up his balloon (glove?) and was walking to the tap when he noticed a small dinosaur on the ground. He quickly picked it up and placed the dinosaur in the glove and refilled it with water. Robert asked me to tie a knot in the glove to secure the dinosaur and water. Robert then manipulated the water, pushing the dinosaur into each finger section of the glove, creating a bubble (Figure 2.7). By doing this Robert noticed that the dinosaur appeared to be 'bigger'. He moved the glove from side to side and kept looking at it in surprise. He then said 'Annette look! it's big, but it's little'.

ANALYSIS AND DISCUSSION

Robert, through his explorations and discoveries was maybe finding out about:

- Weight – Robert could actually see the fingers in the rubber glove elongate with the weight of the water.
- Force – By pushing the water into one of the fingers, the finger changed into a balloon shape.
- Magnification – The dinosaur was magnified by the water and appeared to be bigger.

At this moment Robert was 'disequiliberated'. He did not expect the water to magnify the dinosaur and was amazed to see what had happened. This was new learning for Robert and he had to' accommodate' this event into his way of thinking. 'Accommodation' is a 'situation, experience, event, which does not fit with what is already known' (Bruce 1997: 187)

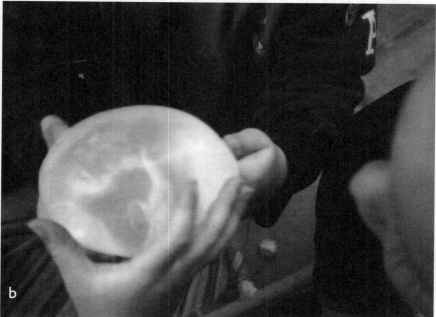

Figure 2.7 (a) Robert fills rubber gloves with water and (b) adds a toy dinosaur.

Robert moves to school

Robert went to 'big school' in September 2002. Both Robert and Susan kept in close contact with the Nursery and often used to visit.

Susan had been part of the Parents Involvement in their Children's Learning (PICL) Study Group at nursery. She then joined the PICL group that was run at Robert's school and supported by Pen Green. At the end of July 2004 Susan designed and produced a portfolio all about Robert called 'Numbers, Numbers Everywhere'. Robert was in Year 2 at the time and was six years and three months old. This is an extract from Susan's portfolio about Robert's interest in growing a sunflower.

The Sunflower

Robert's class recently planted sunflower seeds and began to watch them grow at school before bringing them home.

Robert and I planted his sunflower in the garden and began to measure it on a regular basis.

He particularly liked it when it was smaller than him and then couldn't wait until it was bigger than him.

We took some photos of it growing and talked about what it'll be like when it flowers. At first Robert thought it would flower quite quickly so was a bit disappointed that it didn't. So he painted a picture of what it will look like once it flowers!

During this observation time I have noted that Robert's love of numbers has progressed greatly and his mathematical development has improved immensely.

Robert's vocabulary and understanding of maths terminology has improved too.

He has a greater understanding of sequences, number order i.e. first, second etc. and also terms such as greater than, bigger than, smaller than etc.

Even though graphs have not been introduced at school yet, I have explained the basic principle of a graph i.e. showing growth in a picture type form. Robert seemed to understand the idea of a graph and I believe this is because he understands and enjoys maths and numbers.

As a parent I have spent time looking at how I can help Robert progress further mathematically.

Some of the resources I have got to assist include a calculator as he loved 'playing' with his dad's, and I have shown him how to use it for basic sums: a stop watch as he loves to time things: a tape measure/ruler so he can see how big things are and lots of games, pens and paper so he can practice saying numbers, counting, writing numbers etc.

In order to show the sunflower's growth we noted the height in a diary at least twice a week and I explained to Robert that it would be a good idea to show its growth on a graph rather than just a list of dates and sizes. After showing Robert what a graph would look like he agreed to help. And here is the finished result.

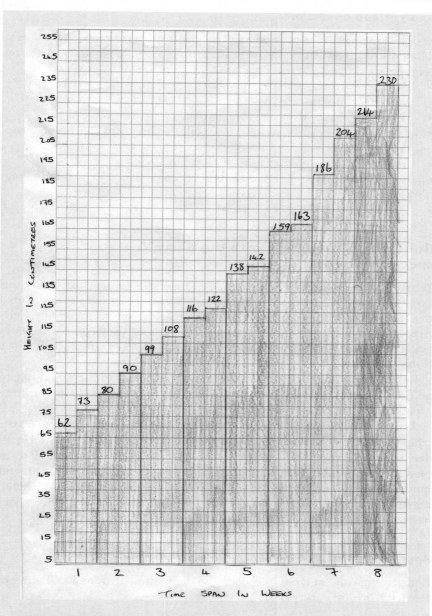

Figure 2.8 Plotting the sunflower's growth.

At the time of completing this portfolio (July 2004), the sunflower is still growing currently 310 centimetres and has still not flowered.

Analysis and discussion

With Susan's involvement at home, Robert was supported and encouraged to develop his interest in the growth of the sunflower. These are some of the concepts we think Robert was beginning to learn about:

- Measurement – linear.
- Height – 'smaller than' and 'bigger than'.
- Time – recording the passing of time in a diary and the simultaneous growth of the sunflower.
- Sequencing – the cycle of growth – seed to bloom.
- Graphs – representing the two aspects of time and growth (a co-ordination of two concepts that are linked).
- Data collection.

Robert's conversation with the Early Years' specialists at age six years two months

Workers at Pen Green were organising a conference on schemas. Susan was asked if she would like to talk about Robert. When she agreed she was invited to a meeting to discuss the conference. The meeting was facilitated by Chris Athey and the aim was to discuss the forthcoming conference. Susan was going to talk about her portfolio of Robert, and I was going to talk about Robert at Nursery.

Robert came to the meeting with Susan. He was asked if he would like to go to Nursery to play but he declined. Robert stayed in the room with the group and began drawing on the flipchart.

Robert produced a wonderful schematic and mathematical drawing on the whiteboard. He had created a graphic representation of the Marriott Hotel, drawing on his recent first-hand experience of staying at the Marriott Hotel in Newcastle. He had included some hotels, his sister, the sun, sky, his car and mum. Most importantly he had placed a sunflower next to the tallest hotel, the Marriott. At this time his sunflower was still growing in the garden, and had still not flowered!

Analysis and discussion

Robert's drawing on the whiteboard also demonstrated an understanding of the mathematical concepts of:

- Division of space – divide the paper up, sub-division of space – makes the windows and panes.
- Height/size
  - He knew the Marriott Hotel was taller than his sunflower.

○   He knew the sunflower was taller than his mum and her car.

○   Robert only had 'partial knowledge' about the other hotels. He believed his sunflower was taller than them.

○   Robert drew his sister taller than himself. He knew she was nine years old and taller than him. (Two related concepts – age and size.)

- Estimation – Robert was estimating that his sunflower was taller than the other two hotels.
- Seriation – The Marriott Hotel was taller than the other two hotels.
- Position – the blue sky, and the sun were positioned at the top of paper. The hotels, the sunflower, his mum and her car were drawn at the bottom of the paper.
- Life cycle – Robert understood that the sunflower needs the sun to make it grow.
- Form – Robert had drawn the buildings in a hard rectangular form and the sunflower with a fluid line. He had also drawn the sunflower without its head.

Schema: Trajectory line, seriation, grid, intersection, enclosure, core and radial.

Susan reflected back on her portfolio and shared the work she had produced about Robert. She then invited Robert to tell the team about the sunflower.

Robert said

My sunflower is bigger than my dad and bigger than the decking. The fence is 200, No! It's 280!

The sunflower is 300 and something 322. Bigger than my dad I like big sunflowers. Uncle Jack's is titchy … smaller than me.

In my street there is a sunflower and it's more than mine and the Granny's is bigger than mine. She's had it for longer. (Two related concepts, size and time.)

Plant a seed, water it and it just grows. Sometimes it bends over we put three pieces of it on (meaning wood supports), you climb up a ladder … I weren't big enough but my mum did.

Dad's measuring tape goes up to 500, the orange one goes up to 200, even more than 200.

When the group broke for a drink and we all went downstairs into the café Robert noticed some cut sunflowers in a vase. He said 'Is it real? Smaller than mine seeds not as big as mine. In winter when it dies you can get the seeds and plant them and they grow. Mine's not got the head' (meaning the flower).

Analysis and discussion – my interpretation

Robert was linking the idea of increasing seriation 'bigger than my dad, bigger than the decking'. Although he said bigger he actually means higher.

He understood that 280 is higher than 200 and that 322 was higher than 300. He also demonstrated that he understood decreasing seriation by using the words 'titchy and smaller than me'.

Robert also acknowledged that the Granny's sunflower was bigger than his because she had had it longer. This clearly illustrated that Robert had an understanding of two concepts: the growth of the sunflower and passing time. This is a co-ordination of two concepts.

Robert then told us about the biological sequence of the sunflower before explaining that the sunflower 'sometimes bends over'. In mathematics this is called a parabola.

He then explained that he had to climb up a ladder but still wasn't tall enough to measure the sunflower. He was thinking about the ladder plus himself, not being as tall as the sunflower. (Addition in his thinking?)

Robert then continued to compare the colour and the size of his dad's measuring tapes giving the exact extended measurement of 500 and 200 and 'even more than 200' – again he used seriation.

He then said that the cut sunflower in the vase was 'smaller than mine, seeds not as big as mine' and again explained the life-cycle of the sunflower, mentioning winter. (Proportionality? Bigger sunflowers have bigger seeds?? Is this his working theory?)

Robert was demonstrating his cognitive understanding of seriation, time, growth and the biological life cycle of a sunflower and could link some of the concepts together. I wonder why Robert was so interested in the growth of the sunflower? Maybe it was because it involved envelopment, going through and trajectory?

Conclusion

I believe that Robert's early exploration of his schemas, envelopment, going through and trajectory at home and Nursery have a strong link to his later mathematical development.

By being observed, listened to, planned for and cognitively challenged, Robert has developed into an autonomous, self-confident, independent learner. He has a strong disposition to learn, his teacher recently told Susan that 'he flies through maths'.

Driven by his 'internal curriculum' (Athey 2005) and by rich first-hand experiences, Robert's mathematical understanding of his world has been consolidated.

Reflections and questions

- Think about Robert's parents and what they gained from knowing about schemas. In what ways did knowing about schemas help them contribute to his learning?
- At what point can schemas be thought of as concepts?
- What seems to be the balance between inner, biological urges and outer, sociocultural stimulation to learn?

Robert and his interests now

Robert is 12 years old (Figure 2.9). He remembers Nursery, especially how he liked to move around, exploring the environment. He also remembers the shaving foam. He is at secondary school and enjoys art, PE and maths. He plays rugby and cricket for a local team and enjoys swimming, playing on his PlayStation and the rollercoaster on holiday.

Figure 2.9 Robert now.

Chapter 3

A case study about Caitlin

Cath Arnold

Introduction

This chapter begins with two memorable observations of children made some time ago. These two observations provide a background to the introduction of Caitlin and her family. Five observations of Caitlin at nursery, made over a period of eight months, are presented in the main body of the chapter. Each observation is presented and then analysed and discussed in relation to Caitlin's exploration of a cluster of schemas, and, when relevant, is also discussed in relation to exploring co-operatively with her friend. To close the chapter, ideas about Caitlin's explorations, links with the curriculum and possible future concepts are drawn together.

Two memorable observations

Observation A

It snowed overnight, so we filled the water tray with snow and brought it into the nursery for children to explore. One little boy, Graeme (aged three), played at the tray all morning using containers, spoons and spades. Inevitably the snow melted. When I noticed that all of the snow had melted, I asked Graeme, 'What's happened? Where is all of the snow?' He replied, 'All the juice has fallen out of it.' (An observation made in a private day nursery.)

Observation B

Christina was drawing a picture. When she had finished, she showed it to me and said 'Mummy, do you want to go into my picture?' I said 'How do you get into the picture?' and she said 'You have to put it on the floor then jump on it,' which we both did. We then pretended we were in the picture. Christina then said 'I want to go back now, so we have to jump on the floor to go back.' We both jumped on the floor and we were back. (An observation made by a parent at home.)

So what?

The two observations above can lead to insights into children's thinking. Graeme's explanation of snow melting comes after a whole morning of freely exploring snow with containers, spoons and spades (the containers have different capacities). Is it any wonder that he has conceptualised the 'juice' (liquid) as being contained in the snow (solid) and then falling out? We do not have a detailed observation of the process but Graeme's actions probably consisted of putting snow into containers and transferring the contents to other containers. After some time the snow being transferred gradually transformed its state from solid to liquid. At the age of three years, Graeme had many earlier experiences of vessels containing liquids and of how liquid can spill or be poured from inside a container to outside. In this instance, he seems to be making an analogy, comparing the solid state of snow to a vessel or container in which liquid is held unless or until it 'falls out'. His conceptualisation might be assisted by the information that molecules are packed tightly together in the solid snow and are less tightly packed and more fluid in the liquid 'juice'.

Christina was trying to solve a different puzzle – how do people get into pictures? Most of us have heard anecdotal stories about young children's ideas about television, that people are actually inside or 'contained' in the box. Christina may have been playing with the idea of people being 'inside' or 'contained' in pictures. Her mother says that they 'pretended' to be inside the picture. This means that Christina may have been using the idea of 'containment' in a symbolic way, with an understanding that you can pretend to be in there but do not really enter by jumping in. Christina also introduces the idea of 'reversibility' in the sense that she suggests 'I want to go back now' (Athey 1990: 41). Graeme made no mention of the reversibility of the liquid 'juice' being refrozen, although with more experience, he might have been able to articulate that process.

The observations of Graeme and Christina have provided instances of children's thinking on which helping adults can reflect. Both of these children revealed their thinking through the actions they carried out and the language they used. In much the same way in this chapter, I am trying to understand Caitlin's thinking and to discover more about how her early exploration of a cluster of schemas contributed to later concept formation.

Caitlin's cluster of schemas included:

- Trajectories – moving in or creating lines in space
- Transporting – being carried or carrying objects from one place to another
- Containing – 'children are fascinated by spaces that *contain* or *envelop*' people, materials or objects (Athey 1990: 149, emphasis in the original)
- Enveloping – children are interested in completely covering themselves, objects or space.

Caitlin was observed over a period of two years at nursery and a predominant schema observed was 'containment'. Athey (1990: 149) says

> Young children are clearly fascinated by spaces that *contain* or *envelop* ... Harris (1975) has reviewed the literature on the evolution of the notion of *envelopment* during the first year and reports that it is only at approximately 12 months that an infant knows that object *a* can occupy the same space as object *b* if *a* is inside *b*. The realization that one object can be inside another is linked to the whole area of object permanence.

'Object permanence' is the idea that objects exist and conserve their features even when we do not directly perceive them or, in other words, cannot see them (Piaget 2001: 118). Athey (1990: 38) states that 'Before *permanence of the object* is well established the child will be distressed if a toy is hidden'. Later on babies and young children play with this idea by playing 'peek-a-boo' and by performing 'magic' tricks.

In this chapter I will draw on examples of Caitlin exploring her 'containment' schema along with a wider, more general cluster of schemas.

Caitlin's home context

Caitlin was born in July 2000. She is bright, sparky, enthusiastic and witty. She was one of the youngest children in her year (with a late July birthday), who was a leader among her group of friends. Caitlin has an older brother, Robert, who displays challenging behaviour and has additional needs. Robert has been diagnosed with Noonan's syndrome, a genetic disorder. Caitlin and Robert live with their mother, Anna. Anna is very interested in her children's education.

Caitlin's nursery context

Caitlin started attending nursery when she was two years, one month and fourteen days. Her Family Worker was Denise, who, during Caitlin's second year, became pregnant and had time off with a problematic pregnancy. After some temporary arrangements, Kirstie became Caitlin's Family Worker. Caitlin made close relationships with both Family Workers.

Caitlin's mother, Anna, had been using services and attending groups at the Pen Green Children's Centre for approximately six years. Robert attended the Pen Green Nursery and the After School Club.

Anna had attended groups at the Pen Green Centre that focused on her children's development and learning for four years and had also attended similar groups in Robert's primary school. Anna has made two portfolios about Robert's interests and has completed a portfolio focusing on Caitlin's interests, entitled 'Caitlin the Explorer' (McColl 2004). In the portfolio, Anna described some of Caitlin's actions:

- Caitlin likes filling objects with water, then lining them in rows from smallest to biggest, then emptying them out and starting again.
- Caitlin loves to dress up and wear lots of make up.
- She also likes to wear high heels and carry handbags, especially when pushing prams. This role play is very important to Caitlin.
- There are photos of Caitlin 'having a bath after covering herself in paint'.

During her first eighteen months attending the nursery, Caitlin developed a strong relationship with Lee. The nature of their relationship is explored through observations presented later in this chapter. Caitlin and Lee were frequently observed playing together in a co-operative way. After eighteen months, the two children grew apart and Caitlin developed a relationship with Megan, who is nine months older than her. Caitlin and Megan began to play together most days. Both Lee and Megan were in the same Family Group as Caitlin.

The focus of this chapter

In this chapter, I hope to show how Caitlin's interest in a cluster of schemas developed. When thinking about Caitlin's relationship with her friend, Lee, Dunn (1993:62–70) finds the following 'dimensions of difference' to be significant:

- affection, enjoyment, caring and support
- connectedness and co-ordination of play
- shared fantasy
- shared humour, gossip and self-disclosure
- conflict, competitiveness and control.

Caitlin was filmed at play on a regular basis at nursery in order to share information and to discuss her development and learning with Anna (Athey 1990; Whalley and Arnold 1997; Whalley 2001;). These video observations are drawn on in retrospect to reflect on Caitlin's actions and thinking.

The first three observations show how Caitlin 'assimilated' different content into her containment schema and 'accommodated' to different ways of filling containers (Piaget 1951 [1962]; Athey 1990). The process of 'assimilation' occurs when a child carries out the same action or set of actions on different materials. 'Accommodation' occurs when a child has to adapt their actions to different materials (Piaget 1951 [1962]). Bruce (1997: 77) explains that 'children try things out according to what they expect and know (*assimilation*) and then adjust, transform and change when things are other than expected (*accommodation*)'.

Observations that link Caitlin's cognitive concerns

Early on at nursery we noticed that Caitlin frequently pushed a buggy and *transported* objects around the nursery. Anna told us that she also *transported* her clothes and other objects around the house. Another very strong interest of Caitlin's was *containing* and *enveloping* objects and materials.

Filling a bottle at the bathroom sink (Observation One)

Caitlin (two years, seven months and twenty-nine days) was trying to fill a bottle at one of the bathroom sinks. The distance between the tap and sink is shorter than the length of the bottle, so Caitlin struggled to position the bottle under the spout of the tap. She was used to placing bottles under the tap to fill them. She experienced a 'disequilibrium' or a gap in her knowledge when the bottle did not fit under the tap (Piaget 1980: 104). She had some help from the adult, who was filming, to prop the bottle at an angle underneath the tap. She noticed that the bottle was not filling up very quickly as only some of the water was going into the bottle. (The water came out of the tap in a *vertical trajectory* and the angle at which the bottle was placed puts the spout at an *oblique trajectory*, therefore some of the water went inside and the rest spilled over the edge.) The adult offered her a strategy for making more of the water go in (placing her finger over part of the spout in order to redirect the flow). Caitlin was focusing on filling the bottle right up.

Analysis and discussion

Caitlin clearly wanted to fill the bottle 'to the top'. Top and bottom are end points in measurement. She knew that she had to place the spout under the flow of water. She had to accommodate to the fact that the bottle would not fit and needed to be placed at an angle. She noticed that the bottle was not filling up quickly and the adult offered her an alternative way of directing the water into the bottle. Caitlin quickly accommodated to this better way of directing the flow. We knew we had offered a psychological 'match' when she adopted this strategy instead of continuing with her previous action or allowing the adult to continue using her finger to direct the water. The adult also offered the information that her finger would be a more effective if she placed it sideways but she did not accommodate to this idea.

Filling a jug with soap and water at the bathroom sink (Observation Two)

Caitlin (two years, nine months and twenty-three days) had just spent a long time (twenty minutes) at the long sink in the nursery. She had been filling jugs and bottles and standing them in a line at the back of the sink. (From a measurement point of view, and considering the 'form' Caitlin was creating, the bottles can be considered to be points in a line, spaces between points, with two end points.) Placing the bottles in these positions demonstrates early knowledge of quantity, length and measurement. The placing of the bottles could also help Caitlin to understand the structure of a sentence, made up of individual words, or the structure of a word, made up of individual letters (Arnold 1999: 45). Caitlin had been observed carrying out similar actions with different content, for example, bowls of sand, blocks and dolls.

Caitlin took a jug into the bathroom and repeatedly used the soap dispenser to put soap into the jug before filling it with water and then emptying the contents into the sink. She talked about the bubbles, watched and felt (by putting her hand in) what happened to the bubbles. Towards the end of the play, she offered the adult a 'coffee'. She discussed whether the adult wanted 'loads' or 'a little bit' or 'a big bit'.

Analysis and discussion

Caitlin was expressing an understanding about the concept of increasing quantity or amount that she had generalised from her exploration of water and was applying to the amount of pretend coffee. It is difficult to know the exact relationship between developing cognitive structures such as *seriation* and experience with water but she was certainly applying her existing knowledge to the pretend coffee situation. She clearly verbalised different quantities that were available. We can also tell from her language about making coffee, that Caitlin was using her cluster of schemas in a 'symbolic' way. Piaget (1951 [1962]: 169) says that a 'symbol ... is an image which has a meaning distinct from its immediate content'. Caitlin was using the water with bubbles as a symbolic representation of coffee.

We can see from Caitlin's actions that she knew the creation of the bubbles was 'functionally dependent' on her putting soap into the jug before filling it up. Her repeated emptying of the contents may indicate a puzzle about what happens to the bubbles when they are tipped out. Do they spread out or disappear?

Caitlin seemed to be experimenting with not only filling a jug with water, but with creating bubbles. She had assimilated the set of actions needed to use the soap dispenser (often younger children can manage to pull the lever that allows the soap to *go through the boundary* but cannot co-ordinate the positioning of a container to *contain* or catch the soap). Caitlin called the mixture 'coffee' towards the end of the play. This symbolic representation may indicate an interest in coffee and how it is made. Anna drinks coffee so Caitlin saw coffee being made at home. Caitlin may know that you put two sorts of 'ingredients' into a container to make coffee. Caitlin also seemed to be interested in the quantity and could differentiate between three amounts offered demonstrating her interest in *seriation*. Athey (1990: 41) says that 'The common-sense world contains sufficient information to feed *seriation structures* such as *size, height, weight, strength, temperature, porosity, number,* and so on'.

Filling buckets with water in the beach area (Observation Three)

Caitlin (three years, one month and thirty days) and Lee (three years, seven months and twenty-one days), her friend, were observed playing in the beach area for over half an hour. Each of them had a hose and they played systematically filling buckets with water. Caitlin used her finger to restrict the flow. The effect was to create bubbles in the water (Figure 3.1).

Figure 3.1 Caitlin with the hose.

Lee put his head into a bucket and licked the water and Caitlin did the same (Figure 3.2).

Figure 3.2 Both children put their heads in the buckets and taste the water.

An adult and another child supplied the children with still more buckets. Caitlin continued creating the bubble effect (Figure 3.3).

Figure 3.3 Caitlin fills more buckets.

When they had filled all of the buckets, Caitlin looked along the line of buckets and said 'We've got two ones, haven't we?' (Figure 3.4).

Figure 3.4 Caitlin reviews her work.

Then she counted '1, 2, 3, 4' (Figure 3.5).

Figure 3.5 The line-up of filled buckets.

Lee dipped his hands into each bucket in turn and Caitlin did the same (Figure 3.6).

Figure 3.6 Lee and Caitlin dip their hands in the buckets.

Then she plunged both arms into the last bucket in the line.

Figure 3.7 Caitlin plunges her arms into the last bucket.

Analysis and discussion

In this sequence Caitlin seemed to co-ordinate her actions observed in the first two sequences. First, she used the idea of placing her finger in the flow of the water, not just to direct the flow (as she did in Observation One) but to increase the speed of the flow resulting in the contents rising and swirling. Caitlin seemed to bring together some of her earlier actions and created a frothy effect in each bucket (as she did with the soap, jug and water in Observation Two). In this instance, Caitlin did not articulate what she was creating. We know from other observations, made at the time, that she was interested in height and speed so the effect of water, speeded-up and directed into a container could be intended to create froth on the surface. Caitlin may have been trying out different ways of creating bubbles in water (other than by putting soap in).

The line of buckets viewed from one end could represent a tool for measuring. In this instance Caitlin was focusing on the 'figural effect' of placing the buckets in a line (what they look like when they are in a line) (Athey 1990: 89). Athey (ibid.) points out that 'Piaget and Inhelder (1956) maintain that marks (and three-dimensional constructions) are the figurative effects of sensorimotor movements'. By reciting numbers, Caitlin was matching her conceptual knowledge of quantity with the figural effect of placing the buckets in a line.

Discussion of co-operative exploration

At this time Lee was not able to use very much expressive language. Caitlin (three years, one month and thirty days) talked to him as though he understood every word (and he appeared to). He used a few sounds with intonation and Caitlin seemed to understand what he meant.

At first glance Caitlin seemed to direct the exploration during the beach sequence. However, on closer examination, the 'connectedness' was more complex and dependent on being able to review the video sequence (Jordan and Henderson 1995). Dunn (1993: 66) points out that 'Measures of "connectedness" in young children are usually heavily dependent on verbal measures. We have not yet made much progress in assessing closeness between young friends when it is expressed nonverbally'.

Although Caitlin *initiated* the filling and knocking over of the first large bucket, Lee *initiated* the pointing of his hose into the air. When the adult in the area brought two more large buckets over, Caitlin filled the other two buckets and Lee continued to fill the first large bucket, demonstrating that he, too, wanted to fill the bucket to the top. When Caitlin said 'Up to the top' and gesticulated by raising her arm above her head, Lee raised his hose and pointed it upwards, as though echoing her gesture in a different way. Lee was first to lick the surface of the water, and then Caitlin tried it. Just after Caitlin had recited '1, 2, 3, 4', Lee intoned '1, 2, 3' as he dipped both hands into each of three buckets. In this instance, he made a *one-to-one correspondence*, while Caitlin looked along a line of buckets and said '1, 2, 3, 4' (there were more than four buckets lined up, so she was not actually counting them but showing she had a sense that these were objects in a sequence which could be counted).

Caitlin immersed her two arms into two of the large buckets and Lee did the same, placing each arm in a bucket in a *one-to-one correspondence*. The water was cold and both children shrieked with laughter while shaking their arms in the air before repeating their actions. Again, the height or depth of water seemed to be a shared interest.

Their vocalisations and gestures show that both children were interested in height and quantity and this may be why they were so attuned to each other in their explorations.

Dunn (1993: 70) says that 'observational work clearly shows that friends do argue and quarrel' and there were moments of conflict between Caitlin and Lee even during the beach sequence. For example, Lee took his watch off when it got wet and gave it to me to look after. Caitlin asked for a turn and Lee immediately protested. At one point, Lee was struggling to take off his jumper and Caitlin wanted to help but, again, he said 'No' emphatically and she accepted his decision. He also shouted 'No' when she wet him when directing her hose.

Towards the end of their play, when all fifteen buckets were full and in two lines (one perpendicular to the other), another boy came and swiftly knocked over six of the buckets and then ran off. Both Caitlin and Lee reacted very quickly. Lee stood each of the six buckets up and Caitlin immediately began filling each in turn using her hose. This was when the pair really worked as a team showing that they both wanted to achieve the same goal.

The whole atmosphere was of fun and enjoyment, a strong feature of close friendships (Dunn 1993: 67). As soon as I started filming, Caitlin involved me in looking at what the two friends were doing. Each of the children had a hose and this meant that they could each carry out their own actions without waiting for a turn. They started off sharing one large bucket but very quickly other buckets were made available. Both children were interested in carrying out similar actions – directing a *trajectory* of water towards a receptacle capable of *containing* the water.

Caitlin seemed to dominate, but when the sequence of events is examined, a great deal of 'reciprocity' is evident (Dunn 1993: 51). Caitlin told Lee where she was in the play twice ('All done, Lee' and 'Lee, I'm finished one'). Dunn (1993: 65) tells us

> To co-ordinate play with a friend, a child must communicate clearly, attend to the perspective of the other, agree more than disagree, delay getting what she herself wants, and manage disagreements so that they do not lead to explosions and can be settled reasonably amicably.

Caitlin noticed the line of buckets and the possibility of counting them. Lee almost echoed the counting by beginning the action of 'dipping both of his hands into each bucket' in a *one-to-one correspondence*. Caitlin then did the same. Lee repeated his actions. They connected with each other through their actions.

In order to conceptually understand how to count, children need to be able to;

> have an understanding of one-to-one correspondence … know that the list of words used must be a consistent one … recognise that the final word has special significance (the total number of items counted) … understand that any items can be counted … know that the order in which items are counted is irrelevant.
>
> (Maclellan 1997: 35–37)

This observation shows that Caitlin and Lee were spontaneously learning and practising different aspects of counting. Caitlin was focusing on the quantity and using the numbers in a stable order, while Lee was practising counting in a *one-to-one correspondence*. The actions of both children were complementary.

An observation in the home area: playing Mummy and Baby (Observation Four)

Many writers and researchers acknowledge the role of pretend play in enabling young children to understand the world of other people (Piaget 1951 [1962]; Barnes 1995; Corsaro 2003; Gussin Paley 2004).

Caitlin (three years, three months and ten days) and Lee (three years, nine months and one day) were filmed in the home area about six weeks after the beach observation. The quality and pace of play in this sequence is different from the beach sequence. At first glance, there may seem few similarities but some of the concepts being explored are similar to those in the previous observations:

Lee was already in bed and Caitlin was saying 'Lee, take your trousers off' and then persuasively 'Because you'll get nice and warm'. Lee took his trousers off and Caitlin got into bed and pulled a cover over both of them. Caitlin said 'Where's my bottle?; and produced a pretend baby's bottle to feed him. (It was one of those bottles that has white liquid in a wall like a flask so you cannot really drink it but it looked authentic.) The bottle was the main prop in their game. Lee played the role of the baby and Caitlin fed him using the bottle. She said 'It's night time, right, no more now, baby'. Both children lay down. Each time after feeding Lee, she put the bottle either under the cover or under the bed. Lee became slightly distracted by two other boys in the area pretending to get ready to go to work. One of them tried to take Lee's wellies as work boots. Lee got agitated and I helped him sort it out.

Lee became interested in the boys' game and started putting his trousers on to join them. Caitlin said 'No, Lee, we're going to bed. It's my turn now. Why did I put your bottle up there?' (The cover had come off and, with it, the bottle). And 'Lee, you can have this pillow. It's nine o'clock ... sssh it's nine o'clock'. In between feeding Lee, Caitlin tried to push the teat into the bottle. She asked Lee and then me 'Do you want this lid?' I said 'No'. (I think she may have seen parents undo the lid and put the teat in upside down to keep it clean.) Caitlin continued trying to dissuade Lee from going off with the other boys saying 'No, you're not going – it's going to be night time'. Lee said 'No'. Caitlin said 'It's going to be night time – it's going to be more dark outside'.

Analysis and discussion

Caitlin and Lee were both interested in being *contained* or *enveloped* by the blanket and the main prop in their game was a *container* (the bottle). The bottle was part way between a real baby's bottle and a symbol. So the appearance was of a bottle with real milk inside but it seemed to come as no surprise to the two children that the milk did not come out. They were using the bottle of pretend milk as a 'symbolic representation' of a bottle of real milk.

When Caitlin told Lee 'Because you'll get nice and warm', she may have been expressing the idea that the heat generated between their two bodies is 'functionally dependent' on their bodies being in close proximity.

After feeding Lee, when Caitlin said 'It's night time, right, no more now, baby', her concern was about quantity. She may have been saying that it is time to sleep or that baby has had enough. The two concepts of time and quantity were being considered together.

Caitlin explored her *containment* schema in a functional dependency way when she placed the bottle under the cover or under the bed to keep it safe – keeping the bottle safe was functionally dependent on keeping it hidden from the view of other children, who may also have wanted to use it.

Caitlin differentiated between night and day, saying 'It's night time' and 'It's nine o'clock'. An interest in *containment* leads to an understanding of *subdivision* of space and time (Dennison and McGinn 2004). Carrying out the actions of placing materials in containers helps children to conceptualise the divisions of space and of time, which are more abstract concepts. Caitlin, again, was expressing an interest in *seriation*, when she said 'It's going to be more dark outside'. The use of the comparative word 'more' shows that she knows that night falls gradually. Caitlin was beginning to show the 'flexibility of thought' described by Miller (cited in Lee and Das Gupta 1995: 29), who says that young children often demonstrate a 'rigidity of thought in the tendency to *focus on states* rather than on the transformations linking states' (original emphasis). We can see from Caitlin's language that she was not rigid in her thinking about day (light) and night (dark) but was beginning to conceptualise the gradual change from day to night.

Although both Caitlin and Lee were interested in *containing* and being *contained*, Lee became quite interested in the boys' play. This was filmed the day after Bonfire Night and two other boys in the home area were playing at being firemen. They were wearing hard hats and wellies and were going off to work. Caitlin showed no interest in wearing a hat or wellies and was very happy with the 'content' she had chosen. Lee, however, became interested in the 'content' of the boys' play and, eventually, went off to join them. Both children continued to be interested in 'containment and envelopment' (the 'form' of children's thinking (Athey 1990: 42)). Children can use different 'content' but be exploring the same 'form'. Arnold (2003) describes Harry making *enclosures* with elastic bands, string and the train track, while his older sister, Georgia (Arnold 1999: 78) explored *enclosures* by making friendship bracelets.

Discussion of co-operative exploration

Faulkner (1995: 259) differentiates between 'fantasy play' and 'socio-dramatic play'. Children engage in socio-dramatic play to understand their lives by echoing 'the content and style of real-life exchanges between adults engaged in similar activities' (p. 260). In order to know how to act out events, children use their knowledge of particular 'scripts' that are within their experience (Nelson 1988). To use this knowledge effectively 'children also have to be able to convey their ideas to each other, negotiate shared meanings, reach agreement about roles, and decide what is to be done in the play' (Faulkner 1995: 259).

The speed with which Caitlin and Lee began to engage in their play suggests that this was a frequently practised scenario for them. Other than the invitation to take his trousers off, Caitlin said very little. At first Lee was a willing baby and Caitlin was able to take on the role of the mummy. This enabled them to be 'affectionate and to care for' each other (Dunn 1993: 62). In her research Dunn (ibid.: 48) found that siblings frequently engage in this sort of play and that children as young as eighteen months can co-operate with the support of a slightly older sibling. Caitlin's comment that 'It's my turn now' meant that not only do they play this game, but that they take turns in being the mummy and baby.

Their positions in their respective families are different. Lee is the older child with a younger sister. Caitlin is the younger child in her family. Each may have played similar games at home with their sibling.

An observation in the discovery area: sweeping the surface of a large body of water (Observation Five)

Two weeks later Caitlin (three years, three months and twenty-eight days) and Lee (three years, nine months and twenty days) were observed in the discovery area. After sweeping water in a puddle (side to side *trajectory* followed by forward and back *trajectory*), Caitlin put the brush end of the broom into the large amount of water *contained* in the barrel and moved it forward and back, away from and towards herself. Her action with the broom head displaced some of the water. She repeated her actions and seemed to deliberately bang the head of the broom against the rim or edge of the barrel resulting in more water being displaced. Then Caitlin placed the head of the broom on the ground and trailed the brush behind her to where Lee was. He too had a small broom. Both children went back to the barrel of water. Caitlin walked with a spring in her step. Each of the children 'swept' the surface of the water. Caitlin 'pulled' the brush towards her displacing water towards herself. Lee 'pushed' the brush away from himself displacing water over the far edge of the barrel.

Caitlin wanted to swap brooms as the head of Lee's broom was a bit bigger, but Lee refused. Caitlin said to me, 'My granny's birthday now'. I said 'Is it?' Caitlin said 'Again'. Caitlin said to Lee 'Not yours'. She went on to say something about 'coming to my granny's birthday'. Both children pushed their brooms away from and back towards them. Caitlin banged hers hard against the edge, shouted and let go and it fell on the ground. Lee shouted and let go of his and it fell to the ground. Both children laughed, picked up their brooms and continued with their game. Both children shouted 'Wooo'.

Caitlin lifted her broom vertically above her head and Lee swept the ground near him. Then she put her broom head into the water and twirled it. Caitlin said 'Lee more ...'. She grabbed his broom and let go of hers. Both children clutched his broom for a couple of seconds. He continued to say 'No'. Caitlin let go and took hold of her broom again. She now thrust her broom as far as it would reach along the channel that feeds the barrel with water a couple of times before pulling it towards herself.

Caitlin went and put her broom head into a large plant pot. She dipped the broom head covered in soil into the barrel of water. Lee joined in. I tried to persuade them not to put soil into the water (because the water is recycled and the soil will clog the filter) but both children continued getting soil onto the bristles and dipping it into the water, making the water darker. Caitlin said 'We want to do it, don't we?'

Analysis and discussion

At the beginning of this sequence Caitlin seemed to be experimenting with using the broom to displace water. At first she moved the brush side to side and found that was not very effective. Then she moved the broom forward and back and discovered that that was a better way of moving the water. She used the broom as an extension of her arm. Caitlin repeatedly used her *trajectory* schema with an interest in functional dependency. Water being displaced from the barrel was functionally dependent on Caitlin's forward and back action. In addition, not getting wet was functionally dependent on using the whole length of the broom handle as an extension of her arm. Another aspect that became intentional after some experimentation, was banging the broom head against the rim of the barrel. The clash of the broom against the rim seemed to make the water jump upwards in a *vertical trajectory*, before falling towards the ground in a *vertical trajectory*. When the water hit the ground, it jumped upwards and outwards, *scattering*.

Her comment about her granny's birthday did not seem to connect, but there may have been a connection with her earlier concern about time. She said 'again', indicating that she remembered her granny's last birthday and that she had some emerging knowledge about how birthdays come around each year. Sweeping with a broom may be something she had seen her granny do, so her own actions might have been making her reflect on what her granny does.

Lifting the broom above her head indicated an interest in where it reached (height) and beginning and end points.

When Caitlin got soil on her brush and dipped it into the water, she was 'transforming' the water by 'performing a different action on it' (Athey 1990: 29). The soil dispersed quite slowly in the large *container* of water.

So now we have observed Caitlin mixing soap and water (Observation Two), sand and water (Observation Three) and soil and water (Observation Five). Each of the materials disperses differently in the water.

Discussion of co-operative exploration

It is obvious that Caitlin liked to be psychologically close or 'connected' to Lee and to share experiences. As soon as Lee moved to join Caitlin, she skipped and smiled and moved quickly back to the barrel and showed Lee what she had been doing.

He did not do exactly the same as Caitlin but their play was 'connected' and 'complementary' (Dunn 1993: 51). It may be because each of them came up with novel ways of extending each other's play that they enjoyed being together.

Lee again 'echoed' Caitlin's actions when she dropped her brush and this became a moment of shared humour, which both children enjoyed. Athey (1990: 75) points out that 'playfulness signifies knowledge that is so well assimilated that it can be played with'.

There were also short episodes of conflict when Caitlin wanted Lee's broom. Dunn (1993: 45) points out that 'Conflicts between friends are just as frequent as those between children who are nonfriends'. Getting into conflict does not necessarily mean not being able to share and co-operate. Isaacs (1933: 221) tells us that

> Any situation in which there is only one thing of a kind, an insufficient number of things for the group, or an assortment of things of varying sizes, will give rise to immediate tension as to who shall have 'it' or 'the biggest'

Isaacs sees it as a human response to such situations. However, Caitlin was not in the position of not having a broom and Lee's was only a bit bigger than hers. She tried to get his and when he asserted himself, she decided to give up, and it did not seem to damage their relationship or the explorations in which they were involved.

She claimed 'ownership' of the birthday of her granny in a similar way, but Lee could not argue about that. Isaacs (1933: 222) says that some children 'felt a keen sense of property in the nursery rhymes and songs they had heard at home ... No-one else had the right to sing or hear these things without their permission'.

Towards the end of the sequence when I tried to dissuade them from putting soil into the water, Caitlin spoke for both of them and their sense of solidarity was communicated.

Conclusion: drawing together ideas

What I have presented in this chapter are only five of the many observations made of Caitlin during her time at nursery. What these observations show are some of Caitlin's and Lee's persistent explorations over a period of time (eight months). Both children showed a consistent interest in containing different amounts of liquid in containers with various capacities, from small bottles to a large barrel. The various containers are the 'content' used and the repeated actions carried out are the cognitive 'form'. Young children really are young scientists, who hypothesise, predict and carry out experiments all of the time in order to find out how the world works (Gopnik *et al.* 1999). Although Gopnik and colleagues (1999: 152) do not mention schemas, they do say that 'babies are actively engaged in looking for patterns in what is going on around them'.

Caitlin's earlier explorations, filling and transferring water from one container to another would almost certainly contribute to her ability to fully understand that the amount of liquid might look different when transferred from one container to another, but unless any of the liquid was added or taken away, the amount stays the same. In order to understand conservation of amount, Das Gupta and Richardson (1995: 5) say,

> Here are three things the child must do at the very least:
>
> 1   mentally represent and 'hold' the transformation (pouring or remoulding) imposed on the materials;
> 2   consider not just how each single dimension (height or width of liquid; length or thickness of clay etc.) has changed independently, but also how they have changed *together* (i.e. how the dimensions are *co-ordinated*);
> 3   compare the consequences of the transformation with the earlier state of the material.

> Caitlin needed to practise over and over again so that she knew from her own experience that the height and width might change when transferring from a tall, narrow container to a short, fat container, but when poured back, it looks and is the same amount.

(Caitlin appears again in Chapter 7 of this book, at school and still concerned with *containing* and *enveloping*.)

Reflections and questions

- Thinking about the investigation with buckets and hoses – what do you think the children's working theories might have been about filling buckets at speed with water?
- During this time of great interest in *containing*, Caitlin and Lee's Family Worker, Denise, was pregnant – what kinds of links could they be making between their play and Denise's pregnancy?
- Caitlin seemed to understand Lee's intentions perfectly well. How might their shared interests have supported their communication?

Caitlin and her interests now

Figure 3.8 Caitlin now.

Caitlin is ten years old (Figure 3.8). She attends the primary school opposite Pen Green. She remembers nursery, especially the home corner. Caitlin is enjoying school. She particularly enjoys climbing, dancing, drama and playing with her friends. She is good at literacy and is currently studying *Macbeth*. She is not so keen on science except carrying out experiments. She is learning to play the clarinet.

Lee's interests now

Lee is ten years old. He doesn't remember anything about nursery. Lee likes dinosaurs and did a project on dinosaurs on the computer. At home, he loves to cook. At school, he likes playing football, doing maths and drawing. He doesn't like drama but does like all the technical stuff backstage. He really dislikes learning to play the trombone.

Chapter 4

A case study about Jack

Angela Prodger

Introduction

In this chapter, I will introduce Jack and include narrative observations, photographic evidence and examples of Jack's work to piece together his cognitive concerns and interests. We have found schemas most helpful in understanding young children and for planning a rich and meaningful curriculum. 'A schema is a pattern of repeated actions. Clusters of schemas develop into later concepts' (Athey 2003). The use of schemas, as a tool for observation, allows us the opportunity to understand the underlying 'form' of actions and representations, make tentative links based on the child's experiences and to plan an individually appropriate curriculum for young children. The case study will consist of information from Jack's home context and relevant information from his time spent in the nursery. Jack showed a deep interest in *trajectories*, *lines* and *connecting* over a period of two years, which culminated in him constructing an umbrella at nursery.

Jack's home context

Jack lives at home with his mum, dad and stepbrother Craig. Jack is the younger of two children. His brother, Craig, was 11 years old when Jack first attended the nursery. Jack was cared for by his mum, dad and maternal grandmother, as his parents both worked. He had attended numerous groups, with his parents and grandmother, at the Pen Green Centre prior to coming in to nursery. Jack and his mother regularly attended a group called Growing Together, which has a particular focus on the parent/child relationship and interactions. When Sue returned to work, she asked her mother to continue attending the group with Jack.

Both of his parents were actively involved in his daily life at nursery. His mother is also actively involved in the local church and the Beavers group in their community. Jack's mother regularly attended a study group at the centre, which focused on parents' involvement in their children's learning. Sue, Jack's mother, was keen to understand Jack's preoccupations and to extend her knowledge about schemas and how these linked with Jack's learning at home and in the nursery.

Jack's nursery context

Jack started in the nursery in September 2001, when he was just three years old. He had a part-time place for his first year in the nursery and during his second year, he attended full-time. He had the same family worker, Michelle, for both years. We felt for Jack that a full-time place in the nursery would offer him more continuity and his parents agreed. During his first month in the nursery Jack used the train track on a daily basis. He liked to construct his own track and his formations became more complex over time. When constructing *lines* and making *connections* with the train track, Jack sometimes showed that he was using his schemas in a symbolic way, allowing one object to stand for another (Athey 2007: 117).

Getting to know Jack

As practitioners, we were able to gather multiple perspectives (Raban *et al.* 2003) about Jack's life and his interests through dialogue with the adults who cared for Jack on a daily basis. Soon after Jack started in the nursery, his family worker, Michelle, observed that he had a cluster of complementary schemas, which he used to help him to make sense of his world. Jack spent endless hours at the train track, *connecting* pieces together and creating *lines* for the trains and carriages to travel along. He would remain involved in his chosen task for up to an hour.

Jack would use the resources in the nursery to fulfil his desire to *line up* and *connect* objects. He used the Duplo cars and connected them to form a horizontal line, before moving them around the environment (Figure 4.1).

Outside, he lined up tricycles and connected trailers to the back, forming yet another line, before riding around the garden. Jack was regularly observed using the hammer at the woodwork bench. Sometimes he would carry out the action, without any product, that is, hitting the hammer on the woodwork bench or a piece of wood without nails and completely involved in the up/down movement. In the gym, Jack enjoyed using the large equipment. He spent time practising his skills on the balancing beam. Once again he was showing his preoccupation with *lines* and *trajectories*, using his whole body to experience this action kinaesthetically.

In early observations at nursery (October 2001), Jack placed numerous lollipop sticks in a vertical position, alongside one another, none of them connecting (Figure 4.2).

Figure 4.1 Jack and the cars.

Figure 4.2 Jack and the lollipop sticks.

He also constructed *vertical lines* using cylinder unit blocks. He was observed gathering planks in the hollow block area and placing them on the floor, parallel to each other in a *vertical line*. Similarly in Athey's study 'Most of the children drew *line-to-line correspondences*, the figurative effect being *parallel lines* or "stripes"' (2007: 91). Jack achieved a similar effect with the planks.

The *lines* that he created could be vertical or horizontal and sometimes the pieces were placed connecting to one another. This could be an early example of Jack experimenting with length and amount.

He also used the dynamic form of *line*, *trajectory* – creating linear movements in space, when using a mallet to flatten clay and when walking across a balancing beam in the gym. Jack also explored and experimented with *enclosures*; he would enclose himself or objects or represent these in his work.

Jack as a learner

Jack was keen to find out things for himself. He was intrinsically motivated. He was an independent thinker and an autonomous learner. Jack would ask for help when he needed it, but would hypothesise and experiment with his own ideas. At times, he would struggle to accept other children's or adults' ideas, as he clearly had his own plan in his mind. By allowing Jack the time and space to discuss his meaning through explanation, negotiation and co-construction, this could lead him 'towards more abstract thinking especially in the domains of literacy and numeracy' (Oers 1997, cited in Worthington and Carruthers 2003: 124).

Building relationships with peers

Over time, Jack developed a trusting and supportive relationship with a child in his family group called Anthony. A family group is a small group of children in a setting with a key worker assigned to them. The group usually consists of no more than eight children per session. Jack and Anthony often worked on their projects together, planning, negotiating and discussing ideas. Dunn (1993: 58) states that

> Some researchers have argued that peer relationships play a special role in several areas of development, including fundamental social skills such as conflict resolution and perspective-taking (e.g. Hartup 1983), moral understanding (Damon 1977) ... and in the development of children's sense of self ... (Sullivan 1953).

The question I would like to pose is 'Did Jack and Anthony choose to play together because they shared similar schemas?' (Arnold 1990). Through focusing on Jack's schemas, both the nursery team and Jack's parents were able to plan ideas to support his learning, making it exciting and challenging for him.

Influences in Jack's immediate environment

Jack noticed lines and intersections in the environment and he would engage adults in a dialogue about these significant landmarks. Jack frequently asked questions about why things happened and how things worked. Jack's home and several other houses nearby were surrounded in scaffolding and had been for many months, whilst necessary renovations were carried out. At his parents' workplace and at the Centre, there was construction work taking place and they, too, had scaffolding in place. His parents shared with his family worker that on a walk up to the nursery from his home, he mentioned the scaffolding on the outside of his home, asking 'How do the men get right up to the top?'

Each day Jack and his carers would go on a bridge over a railway line on the way to nursery. He asked to be lifted up to view the railway tracks as they crossed over the bridge. When an ambulance passed, he commented that it had a cross on like his church. From this observation, we can begin to make tentative links with Jack's interest in lines and how lines can be connected to form extended vertical, horizontal or oblique lines and arranged to form intersections or *grids*. Jack repeatedly observed these types of structures in his environment and began to represent similar constructions in his play.

Observation with the trains and track at nursery

Jack (three years, two months) was lying on his front along the floor, gaining a different view of the trains and track. Jack accompanied his play with sounds and language, as he moved engines and carriages along the track and through tunnels. Jack named the engines after the character engines from *Thomas the Tank Engine*. He moved cars along a plank and said that 'Daddy's gone to work' (Figure 4.3).

Analysis and discussion

Jack seemed to be exploring *trajectory*, *connection* and *going through a boundary* in his actions with the trains. We know that Jack had first-hand experience of engines and carriages as he frequently stopped at the railway bridge, to observe the daily rail freight passing through, as he walked up to nursery. Naming the engines showed that Jack was using the trains at nursery to symbolically represent the characters in the *Thomas* stories he loved. His conversation about his dad going to work also indicated that he was using symbols to represent and think about his dad's journey (a *trajectory*) by car.

Figure 4.3 Jack's lines of cars on a plank.

At home

At home, Jack liked to carry out small projects. He often constructed three-dimensional models from scrap materials that he found around his home. He also enjoyed participating in real work, outside in the garden with his dad. He enjoyed moving large lengths of wood around the garden. He loved to hammer nails into pieces of wood and connect objects together using lengths of string, rope or sticky tape. His mum shared with us that she frequently had to visit the local supermarket, late at night, as Jack had run out of sticky tape and was refusing to go to bed until he had finished his construction.

Jack's parents supported his interest in *lines* and *connections*. His parents offered him lots of open ended resources, e.g. sticky tape, drinking straws, cardboard tubes and household recycled waste. Jack constructed many 3D models, e.g. binoculars, a guitar, crosses for church, and swords. The similarity was in the 'form' he was creating each time. Jack continued to be fascinated by the scaffolding around his house. He frequently observed the workmen making their way through the scaffolding. He was also curious about how the poles connected and where they led.

At nursery

Using paper, tape, lollipop sticks, junk, elastic bands and straws, Jack has constructed a kite, flute, guitar, a giant, binoculars and an umbrella (Figure 4.4).

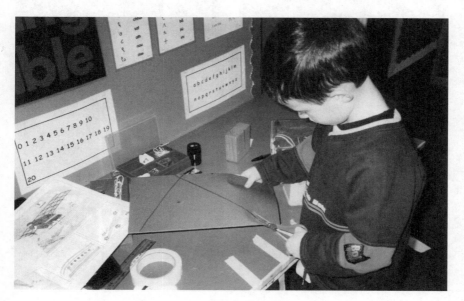

Figure 4.4 Jack's construction projects (continued overleaf)

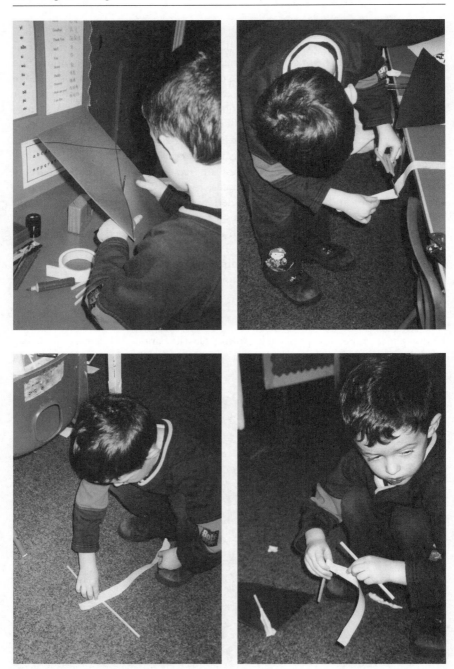

Figure 4.4 Jack's construction projects.

Analysis and discussion

Was this Jack's attempt at turning his internalised thoughts into actions that could be shared with others? Could this have linked to the scaffolding that had been erected around his home, whilst some exterior work was carried out? From Jack's perspective of the scaffolding, he would observe many poles in the vertical position as he walked to and from his home. At this early stage, Jack did not always articulate his ideas, but he repeatedly showed us what he was curious about through his actions, representations and through his questions. Was he trying to understand the relationship between the horizontal and vertical poles in establishing intersections?

Jack usually constructed with a purpose in mind, He was often engaged in a 'silent narrative' (McGinn 2003). During these periods he showed high levels of involvement and would persist for extended periods of time. I believe that during these periods of engagement, Jack was intrinsically motivated, which leads to 'deep level learning' and in turn results in higher order thinking (Laevers 1997: 18).

When observing Jack over time, these dominant patterns (schemas) were clearly visible to the practitioners in the nursery team and Jack's parents. It was important when co-constructing with Jack that we offered him appropriate language to support his actions. Although Jack was repeatedly carrying out these schemas, he did not always use language to articulate his actions. He frequently asked questions, which linked directly with *lines*, *trajectories* and *connections*, for example, 'Can you make a big, long one?' 'Why do the workmen go up, up and up to there?' and 'Where does the water go when it goes down the drain?' His language reflected his concern with *up/down* and *going through*.

Making a flute (aged four years and four months)

One of Jack's projects that he was particularly proud of was a flute. It was a wonderful creation, which showed his skill and knowledge of *lines* and *connections*. Jack had mastered how to use sticky tape effectively to form secure connections and to construct intersections. His fine motor skills were becoming more developed through practice. He was able to work on a much smaller scale than previously. Jack used drinking straws and sticky tape. He cut several drinking straw into fairly equal parts. Jack then *connected* these parts with sticky tape to make the body of the flute. He then snipped some smaller parts from the straws and connected them at right angles along the body of the flute (Figure 4.5). Once again these pieces were placed with precision. Jack obviously had a clear plan his mind about how his flute should look.

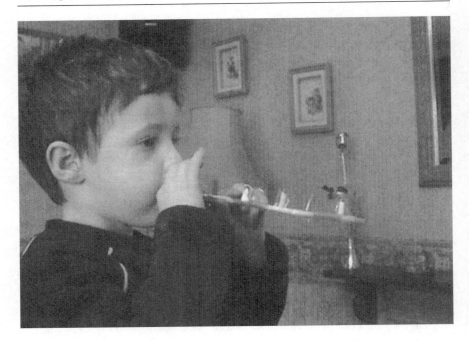

Figure 4.5 Jack's flute.

Analysis and discussion

Jack seemed to be representing what a flute looked like to him. He transformed his raw materials (straws) into equal lengths, showing his knowledge of division. Then he used the parts to create a whole flute. He seemed interested in making parts into a whole object, adding on to increase the length and *enclosing* with sticky tape to *connect* and strengthen. He already knew how to construct and strengthen the body of the flute using straws and sticky tape. He then repeated his action of dividing, to create the means to play the flute, placing the small pieces of straw along the flute at regular intervals.

What we are unsure of is whether Jack understood how a real flute worked. Was he trying to create a wind instrument and had he selected straws in the knowledge that he could blow through them to create sound?

Documenting children's learning

In order for us, as practitioners, to understand Jack's cognitive concerns, it was vital that we systematically documented his learning. Jack's time in the nursery has been documented in his 'Celebration of Achievements' file. This record consists of narrative observations, photographic evidence and examples of his work showing summative assessments and individual progression over time. The file is an ongoing record of achievement. Parents, children and colleagues are encouraged to add information to the file to build a comprehensive record of the child's learning both at home and in nursery.

Jack often brought past experiences and prior knowledge to his current play. He would try out similar actions, assimilating new ideas, using a range of resources that were available to him in the nursery.

Representing home experiences at nursery

Jack (four years and four months) had been to the local theatre with his parents, to watch a production of *Jack and the Beanstalk*. When he returned to nursery, he wanted to re-tell the story of *Jack and the Beanstalk*. He selected resources and set about making a Giant. He used an oval piece of paper to draw the Giant's face. He then connected several art straws together with masking tape to construct the long body of the Giant. Jack asked for the Giant to be fixed to a high point in the nursery. This allowed him to observe the vertical line and to view the height from below.

Analysis and discussion

There was no doubt that the experience of going to see *Jack and the Beanstalk* and particularly the Giant had matched Jack's interest at that time. This time, he used art straws (longer than drinking straws and more pliable) to construct the body of his Giant, once again making a long *line* by adding on and *connecting* together the straws. He also used masking tape, which was a bit stronger than sticky tape for this larger project. By now, Jack was becoming very skilled in choosing and using the materials available to him, but he had also co-ordinated several schemas, *lines*, *enclosing*, *connecting* and *on top*. He drew the Giant's face on a large oval piece of paper and placed it at the top. He was clearly fascinated by looking up and seeing the sheer height of the giant onstage and that may also have been something that excited Jack about the scaffolding he had viewed at close quarters.

Working with his friend Anthony

As Jack gained a fuller understanding of *lines* and *trajectories*, he was able to create more complex constructions. Jack would work with his friend Anthony in the hollow block and unit block area. They frequently constructed props for their play. They made a kennel, which was composed of a three-sided construction, where the hollow blocks were placed, side by side and on top of one another, with precision in straight lines. Finally a roof made from planks was placed on top. The front was left open to allow the boys access into the kennel.

Both boys worked together. At times Jack would move a block that had been placed by Anthony and place it where he wanted it to be. Jack often led the play and learning opportunities and on occasion would get frustrated, as he was not always able to articulate his intended ideas to others.

An observation in the maple block area

Jack (four years and eight months) and Anthony had been building in the maple block area. Jack had a paper and pencil and was making a drawing from a series of photographs of Anthony's building on the wall in the block area (Figure 4.6). I asked Jack what he was drawing and he told me 'It says how we build Anthony's building.'

Anthony and Jack started to recreate the building in the photographs using unit blocks, laying unit blocks in turn (Figure 4.7).

Jack and Anthony built on the carpet outside of the block area towards the home corner, *connecting enclosures*.

Anthony to Jack:	Come on, I'm building outside. (They were synchronising their actions.)
Jack:	Anthony, that's what you did, didn't you? Do you think we just need to do that? (Jack pointed to a particular photograph.)
Anthony:	Yes (nodding).
Jack:	Copying same as that.
Anthony:	Not allowed a go that way, if someone trips over it, it's not their fault.
Jack:	What else did you do, Anthony?

Analysis and discussion

When using the unit blocks on this occasion, Jack and Anthony constructed a network of roads. The complexity of this construction included horizontal lines, oblique lines, intersections, arcs and enclosures, created by placing blocks with precision. The pair worked with synchronised actions and a shared understanding. Each block was placed in turn and negotiated if necessary. During this period of construction, Jack would stand back to observe and reflect on their design so far. Jack was able to demonstrate that he had a vast knowledge about lines and connections and he could use this to enrich his play and enhance his constructions. Jack was able to use visual clues,

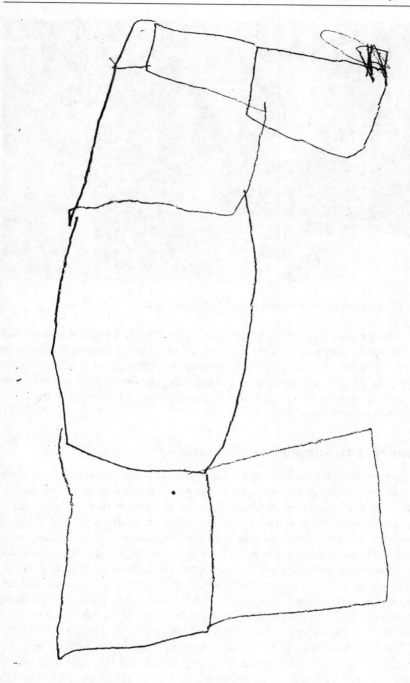

Figure 4.6 Jack's building plan.

Figure 4.7 Jack and Anthony setting out the building in blocks.

e.g. photographs, designs and concrete examples. Jack and Anthony had become strong play partners. As the boys acquired more language, they were able to negotiate ideas and their relationship was more equal in terms of each leading the play at different times. During this experience, Jack and Anthony explored the concepts of length, shape, design, maps, division of space, area, angles and communication.

Resources to support Jack's thinking

It is important that children have a wide range of resources available to them and that they have the opportunity to use these in the way that they choose, which may not be the way in which adults might expect them to be used.

It became apparent that Jack's play was often on a large scale and involved movement. Within a free-flow play environment, Jack was able to move freely around the nursery, finding objects and resources that he was able to use to enable him to assimilate his ideas about *lines, trajectories* and *connections* (Figure 4.8)

At home he was also seeking out and using objects to line up and connect, to try out his hypotheses and challenge his thinking further still. I believe that through Jack's rich experiences of lines, he now had a great understanding about lines in their vertical, horizontal and oblique form. He knew that lines could be formed upwards, downwards, from side to side and diagonally. He knew that they could intersect at right angles and that he could make stress points stronger by binding or *enclosing* joints with sticky pliable materials such as sticky tape or masking tape.

Figure 4.8 Jack plays on a large scale, drawing together different resources.

Increasing complexity

As Jack's constructions became more complex, he began experimenting with more refined fine motor movements. He would repeatedly unravel till rolls and sticky tape to create *lines*. The process was of great importance to him. I believe that Jack needed first-hand experience of this process, to understand how to go on to use sticky tape in an effective way. He also showed an interest in mark-making at the graphics area. He used pens and straight edges to draw lines and create intersections. He soon began to form *zigzags* and often represented this in his mark-making. Jack was attracted to the graph paper and the bingo tickets, when they were available in this area. Was this because of their *grid*-like form and his interest in linear formations?

Shadows

Jack's mother, Sue, told us about how Jack always noticed *lines* and *intersections* in his local environment and how he could use this in a humorous way.

Observation on the way to nursery

One day on a journey to nursery, Jack noticed his own and his mum's shadow on the path. His mum's shadow stretched out on to the road. He alerted her attention to this and commented that she would get run over. He then laughed out loud.

Chris Athey says that only when a child knows something well, can they be playful with their knowledge. This is our evidence that Jack now had a good understanding and working knowledge about *lines* and *trajectories*, as he could use this knowledge with humour.

At a similar time in the nursery, Jack was using art straws, lollipop sticks, balsa wood and masking tape to make crosses, swords, kites and giants. Jack was now regularly including mark-making in his play. He was beginning to understand that he could communicate his ideas to others through representation in its three-dimensional form, verbal communication and mark-making.

Jack continued to make props for his play. He made a firefighter hose from straws and a large cardboard tube; he poured water through the tube using a watering can. He also experimented with a real hose outside on our beach to make a river. Jack made great use of all opportunities, by taking what was of interest to him, fitting it into this current thinking to enhance his already extensive knowledge of *lines*, *trajectories* and *connections*.

Bringing all of his knowledge together to make an umbrella

Jack (four years and eight months) worked in close partnership with his family worker, Michelle, to construct an umbrella. The idea came from him. Michelle offered him support by finding a picture of an umbrella, as well as teasing out and acknowledging his own internalised thoughts and ideas. Jack was deeply involved and persisted for a long period of time to carry out his plan. This was an ambitious project for a four-year-old, but it did not appear to faze Jack. He had a clear plan in mind and he had already gathered the resources that he had chosen to use for this project. The resources consisted of card, masking tape, art straws, Pritt Stick, scissors, lollipop sticks and pens.

Jack began with a large piece of green card. He was not satisfied with his initial attempts to form a circle for the canopy of the umbrella. Michelle was there to subtly intervene and reminded Jack of a previous time, when he had constructed a kite. On this previous occasion, Jack had folded the paper in half and drawn intersecting lines on it, before cutting it out to create an almost symmetrical kite shape. Jack listened carefully and appeared to accommodate this idea. He drew on his prior knowledge and experience and immediately continued with his work. He folded the green card and drew an arced line (semicircle) on the card with support from Michelle. Jack was competent in using scissors. He was able to follow the line and cut out a shape that he was pleased with.

Jack looked closely at the circle that he had made. He then moved on to construct the handle for the umbrella. Jack had selected straws for this process. Jack was an expert in using straws to create props. He also knew how to use them in a variety of different ways. For this project, he had chosen to use art straws. He carefully manipulated the straws by twisting one end and then gently forcing this inside the end of another straw. This was an intricate process, which required precision and concentration. He did successfully connect the straws, but he was dissatisfied with the result, as they were not secure enough and lacked strength. At this point, Jack was disequilibrated, as his idea had not gone to plan. Michelle asked Jack if he had any ideas about how he could make his *connection* more secure. Jack's immediate response was 'Sellotape'. He reached out for the masking tape and began unravelling the roll and wrapping the tape around the joints. This was more satisfying for Jack as the connections did not easily become disconnected and they appeared to be much stronger. He repeated this process of binding (*enveloping*) each connection with masking tape. When Jack had completed this, he once again took some time to reflect on his work so far. Jack decided that it could be modified and he selected several lollipop sticks and began to connect them to one end of the straw shaft. He was keen to create an arced line using the lollipop sticks, to represent a curved handle. Jack manipulated the sticks once he had connected them together with masking tape. When he had mastered his desired design, he had to consider how he would connect the handle to the canopy, which he had created earlier. At the same time in nursery, Jack was experimenting with writing 'J' for Jack. He often practised this or offered to write his own name on his pieces of work. Here, we were able to observe similar patterns being demonstrated in Jack's three-dimensional work and his attempts at making meaningful marks.

Jack and Michelle talked about how Jack could connect the handle to the canopy. Jack decided that he would use scissors to snip a hole in the centre of the canopy and then push the straws through. Michelle offered Jack some guidance on how he could achieve this and once again Jack was able to listen to the advice and carry out the process. He cut the hole in the card and forced one end of the straw handle through the hole. Jack secured this connection with masking tape. On completion, Jack raised the umbrella into the air, as if to share his moment of pride, but he looked quite disappointed. The plan had not turned out as he had hoped. He said, 'Oh, it's all floppy.' Michelle agreed with Jack and they looked at his design together. Michelle showed Jack the umbrella in the book that she had brought along. They closely observed the umbrella spokes and studied the formation.

Jack began work again. He understood that he needed some support for the canopy and he chose to use lollipop sticks to strengthen it. He placed the canopy onto the floor and taped the first lollipop sticks on to the card. Jack continued around the circle positioning each lollipop stick an equal distance apart. Once all of the sticks were in place, Jack secured each one with an additional piece of masking tape. At last his umbrella was complete and he raised it in to the air and walked the whole length of the corridor back in to the nursery to show everyone his wonderful achievement.

Analysis and discussion

During this process Jack showed that he was able to create and use horizontal, vertical and oblique lines. He has also used arced lines, therefore he understood that lines did not have to be straight. He was able to use a line from a fold in a piece of paper to enable him to create a symmetrical shape. An emerging schema from this project was *core with radial*, as Jack constructed the spokes for the canopy of the umbrella.

Jack had frequently subdivided space in other props he had made, but this was different and more complex as it involved creating a central *core with radials*, that created panels of an equal size. Whereas he had previously mastered placing materials at right angles to each other, dividing a circle into four equal parts, here he was experimenting with dividing a circle into a larger number of equal parts.

Conclusion

This case study of Jack seemed to show clearly how his 'environmental circumstances were supplying encounters for him which permitted him to use the repertoire of schemas that he had already developed' (Hunt 1961: 279). He constantly sought out new 'content' to assimilate to the schemas he was interested in. His parents and workers were tuned in to his needs and interests and were also attempting to match his interests.

On at least one occasion, Jack was 'disequilibrated' by what happened. He seemed to think he could make a strong enough shaft for his umbrella by using the technique of inserting one straw inside another. The result was too floppy. He already seemed to know how to strengthen the shaft, showing that he was co-ordinating several schemas.

Jack constantly challenged himself and became a great solver of problems. He also became socially adept by negotiating plans with his chosen play partners, sometimes adults and sometimes other children. These dispositions were sure to serve him well in the future.

Reflections and questions

- Jack's parents went to great lengths to support his investigations. How do you think he felt when, what he was interested in was supported by so many other people?
- What is the difference between a themed approach ('Let's all make umbrellas') and Jack's experience of making an umbrella at nursery?

Jack's interests now

Jack is 11 years old (figure 4.9). Jack doesn't remember much about nursery except he can remember making a sword from wood and sticky tape and also remembers making a wrestling ring from the bricks with his friend, Anthony. He says, 'Anthony jumped on top of me when we'd finished!'

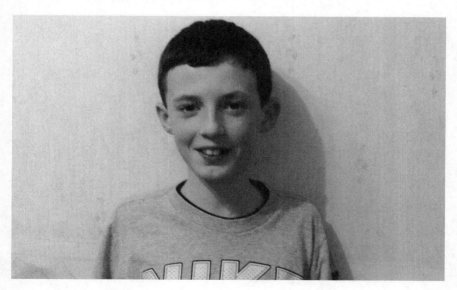

Figure 4.9 Jack now.

Now he quite likes ICT. He has built his own website and likes doing video and photography and sometimes puts them on YouTube. He likes collecting things, cards and snow globes. He still likes making things and doing models. He makes model aeroplanes and hangs them in his room.

Chapter 5

A case study about Steffi

Katey Mairs and Cath Arnold

Introduction

In writing this chapter about Steffi, we have the privilege of extensive records which document her interests and concerns over a two-year period in nursery. She explored these interests through her repeated and coherent patterns in play (schemas). Our knowledge has been enriched through dialogue with her parents about her play experiences at home. Steffi's development of mark-making had been the focus of a small research project and, from this, we have video of Steffi both in nursery and later in her reception year at school.

Home context

At this time Steffi lived with her two older sisters, Brogan and Holly, mum, Jackie, and father, Mark. Jackie is a passionate gardener and has a keen interest in and knowledge about the natural world. Jackie worked in a local care home for the elderly and involved Steffi in visiting the residents on a regular basis. Mark shared his enthusiasm for stories and role play with Steffi at home. Their favourite shared story was *The Lion, the Witch and the Wardrobe*.

Nursery context

Steffi attended nursery on a part time basis from the age of two years, ten months until she started infant school at the age of four years, ten months. Her nursery file 'A Celebration of My Achievements' documents how carefully she made choices from a range of resources within the nursery environment to support her dominant schemas in order to pursue her interests and cognitive concerns. She also demonstrated her ability to choose the appropriate play partner (adult or child) to share her play experience or develop her interest. From three years, two months, Dana was her 'special' friend with whom she shared an interest in animals and dinosaurs. Through her role play with animals she explored a number of mathematical concepts:

- size seriation (sorting from small to medium to large)
- spatial order (placing animals in an order, filling space)
- position and proximity (placing animals in different positions from which she could see things differently)

By the age of three years, eleven months, Steffi was choosing to play with Hamish. Both children had assimilated a sophisticated understanding and knowledge of the meaning of words to such an extent that they were able to be 'playful' with them. For example, they would be interested in words that rhymed, such as 'rose' and 'nose'. Chris Athey described this 'sound similarity' as 'pre pun', noticing a difference in two words with similar sounds. When we learn to use a pun (proper), there is a perceptual similarity but a conceptual difference in meaning. So, one word can convey two different meanings and can be used humorously (Athey 2006).

Steffi's Key Worker, Margaret, supported their emerging knowledge of language and meaning by writing down their stories, reading them stories and humorous poems and rhymes. When Steffi wanted more active play, she chose to play with a group of boys who were frequently involved in chasing games (*dynamic trajectory*).

Steffi's schemas

Steffi used her schemas in both a dynamic (moving) and configurative (still) form to help her accommodate new ideas about:

- What is underneath or inside what I can see?
- What does 'being dead' mean?
- What does it feel like to be a leader, powerful and brave?
- What is a family?
- How can I transform myself and the materials in my environment?

Steffi's first year at nursery

From the records of Steffi's first year at nursery, we will focus on her use of *enclosing*, *containing* and *enveloping* schemas, which cluster as she builds her knowledge about her interests and concerns.

A first observation

Steffi started nursery at the age of two years and ten months. Her dad accompanied her for the two-week transition period from home to nursery. The first written narrative observation in her recordkeeping documented Steffi's play at the dough table, with Mark involved in her play.

Steffi was dividing the dough with her hands and putting pieces into a saucepan. Mark reached out and offered her some paper cake cases. Steffi then sub-divided the dough and put one smaller piece of dough into each cake case.

Analysis and discussion

Steffi began using her *containing* schema to explore the mathematical concept of *one to one correspondence*. Athey (1990: 193) says 'Although schematic behaviours are obvious, worthwhile curriculum extensions do not immediately suggest themselves'. Perhaps, intuitively, Mark had intervened to develop Steffi's knowledge of number, amount and division. Maclellan (1997: 35) states that the 'one to one principle' is the first counting principle of five principles that young children need to co-ordinate in order to fully understand how to count.

An observation of Steffi painting at the easel

Shortly after starting nursery, Steffi used just two colours (red and yellow), making up/down movements (*trajectory*) and circular movements (*rotation* and *enclosure*). Steffi covered (*enveloped*) one colour with the other (Figure 5.1).

Analysis and discussion

Steffi was very involved in experimenting with the two colours. She was seeing the figurative effect of her *trajectory* and *enclosing* or *rotating* movements. She was also seeing the effect of covering red with yellow and then with red again, a kind of *enveloping* and *layering* of coats of paint. She seemed interested in transforming the colours and possibly in creating a new colour or shade. In this case, she knew what was 'underneath' although she was unable to reverse the process.

Observations using the dough

Steffi continued to use the dough often. At two years, ten months, she sliced up a lump of dough and stuck matchsticks into it. She said 'It's a rhino'. She then took the sticks out and flattened the dough before sticking the matchsticks in. An adult observing said 'It looks like a hedgehog'. She agreed.

A month later (at two years, eleven months) Steffi made a 'birthday cake' by placing coloured sticks into a lump of dough.

Analysis and discussion

The examples above show how Steffi was exploring a particular 'form' or schema, usually referred to as *core with radial*. Although she was quite young and unlikely to draw or write just yet, nevertheless she was interested in

Figure 5.1 Steffi painting.

co-ordinating her *enclosure* and *trajectory* schemas. Steffi was representing 'content' she was interested in (rhinos and hedgehogs) and/or familiar with (birthday cake).

A drawing

A year later (at three years, eleven months) Steffi was still exploring a *core with radial* form, but by this time, she was expressing her ideas in drawing (Figure 5.2):

Analysis and discussion

Steffi was demonstrating her knowledge of other 'content' (spiders) that have a similar 'form'. She was also showing an interest in spiders eating (or *containing*) flies and possibly trapping them in webs.

Being 'inside' or enveloped

There are many examples of Steffi bringing her two strong interests (animals and enveloping) together by dressing up in animal costumes and wearing animal face paints (Figures 5.3 and 5.4).

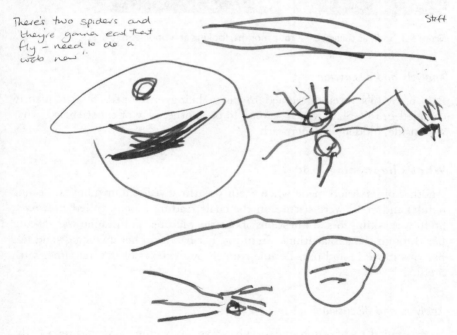

Figure 5.2 Steffi's spider drawing: 'There's two spiders and they're gonna eat that fly – need to do a web now'.

Figure 5.3 Steffi at three years, four months, looking at a book about tigers.

Analysis and discussion

Part of Steffi's interest seemed to be in being enveloped. She frequently engaged in role play, which seemed to be another way of experiencing what was inside, hidden or underneath.

What's happening inside?

Another observation made when Steffi was three years, four months. Leanne (adult) and Steffi were sitting on the chair reading a book called *Breathing*. Steffi was asking lots of questions about the pictures and Leanne was talking her through the explanations. Steffi put her hands on her own chest and felt her ribs move in and out. Leanne read through the book several times with Steffi.

Analysis and discussion

Steffi seemed to be interested in what was happening *inside* her own body. This also may have linked with her interest in death and with her question 'What is dead?'

Figure 5.4 Steffi at three years, five months playing with slime at the water tray.

Playing with the animals and dinosaurs

At three years, eight months, Steffi was using the animals and dinosaurs in nursery on a daily basis. She sorted them into sets and sub-sets. The sub-set became part of a role play which usually involved daddy, mummy and baby.

Analysis and discussion

Steffi was classifying animals as male and female. She was interested in whether animals were 'fierce' or not. She was making choices from the environmental content and her schemas to assimilate how objects might be *classified* and *seriated*.

Steffi's second year at nursery

During Steffi's second year at nursery, she continued to build on her earlier learning by co-ordinating her schemas and following three main interests:

- What's inside or underneath and combining materials that transform when put together
- Drawing and writing using symbols
- Learning about families and being strong using animal figures

What's Inside? and transforming materials by putting them together

Playing with dough again

When Steffi was three years, ten months, she had had many experiences in nursery of acting on a range of malleable materials, for example, flour, cornflour, slime, shaving foam, sand and soil. She had assimilated a broad range of materials into her cluster of schemas and had a sound knowledge of how materials transform when mixed with other materials. Her Family Worker recorded:

> Steffi followed the recipe for dough and made it from start to finish. She was more interested in making it than playing with it. She showed an interest in counting out the amounts needed. She used number names accurately. She asked for 'more flour to fill the cup'. She described the consistency of the dough as 'too sticky' and added more flour.

Analysis and discussion

Steffi now had a strong interest in the process of mixing materials. She had an understanding that amount was important to the outcome and that she could reverse the outcome. When she realised that the dough was 'too sticky' she requested 'more flour' to achieve what she has experienced as the right consistency. By being introduced to a recipe and the idea that exact amounts are needed to produce a required outcome, Steffi was now operating her thought processes to think through and decide what was needed to make the mixture the right consistency (of which she had enough experiences to assess).

Steffi seemed to understand that some processes were reversible, which is essential for understanding 'conservation'. She had now gone beyond the mental and physical actions of grouping together, as she had repeatedly done with animals and dinosaurs, to begin to understand the mathematical operation of addition. She realised that the action of grouping together, in this case the amounts required for making dough, could also be cancelled out or reversed by adding more flour. Steffi appeared to have internalised the notion that amounts added together produce a specific outcome and that, by adding more or less of one ingredient, this will create a different outcome. She showed that she was beginning to work on the stuff that contributes to understanding the concepts of addition, subtraction and simple algebra.

Playing with clay

Three weeks later Steffi was using clay and water, adding water to the clay. She talked about the clay being 'slidey and slippy' and 'cold and squashy'.

Analysis and discussion

Clay feels very different to dough and adding water transforms the clay and makes it more pliable. Steffi seemed to be building on her experience of putting materials together to make them behave and feel differently. In this instance she was able to articulate, in language, how the clay felt in her hands. Her language focused on the actions of her hands, that 'slide', 'slip' and can 'squash' the clay. Here we can hear Steffi using alliteration (the occurrence of the same letter at the beginning of adjacent or closely connected words) and onomatopoeia (the formation of words from sounds associated with what is named or described). Alliteration and onomatopoeia are forms or structures of language used to communicate how something sounds and feels. This use of language was extremely sophisticated.

Making Angel Delight

Three weeks later, at four years, two weeks, Steffi followed the recipe on the pack and made Angel Delight. She reflected on the process, saying 'I was making jelly-cake and I put it in the oven'.

Analysis and discussion

By then, Steffi was not only aware of combining ingredients for a specific outcome, but also she was beginning to understand that we can communicate symbolically with each other how to reach that outcome. Although she could not read, she could follow instructions and she knew that certain amounts of materials could result in certain outcomes. Her own language about what she was making reflected her understanding that the final product was like jelly and like a cake. She also mentioned 'putting it into the oven' showing a sense of understanding other ways that transformations take place, that is, by heating the mixture. In this instance, she probably put the mix into the fridge to set, an almost opposite process of cooling down.

Looking at What's Inside?, a factual book

When Steffi was nearly four years, three months, her Family Worker introduced a book entitled *What's Inside?* a book about pregnant mammals and other creatures. Margaret reported that 'Steffi was visibly delighted and wanted to look through it before storytime. She loved the illustration of the pregnant horse. She was really chuffed to be able to take it home.'

Analysis and discussion

This seemed to feed into Steffi's interest in understanding what's inside that we cannot see. It must be very difficult for a young child to conceptualise a baby *contained* inside a tummy, especially when the animal is as big as a horse.

Other opportunities for Steffi to learn about What's Inside?: gutting a fish

When Steffi was four years, three months, her Family Worker brought a trout into nursery to gut and cook.

> Steffi was fascinated by the whole process and watched intently as Courtney spread out the guts with a spoon and Hamish took its eyeball out, telling us it looked like a button. She was most interested in the guts and bones. We took the bone out in one piece and had a good look at it' (Figure 5.5)

A few weeks later when Steffi was four years, five months, she asked Margaret when she was going to bring in another fish. Margaret did and reported, 'She studied it closely, particularly the mouth and gills – at lunch she had some on her plate (not sure if she ate it though)'. Steffi did not want to handle the trout but said the best bit was 'cutting its head open' and she could 'see part of its brain'.

Figure 5.5 Steffi and friends study the fish.

What's underground?

The same day, Margaret introduced a new book to Steffi, which she loved and was knowledgeable about. It was called *Underground* and had see-through pages so that on either side of the page you could see how animals lived above and below ground.

Analysis and discussion

The three observations above illustrate some of the opportunities on offer that appealed to Steffi at this time. The form she was interested in was *containing, enveloping* and *insideness*. Gutting a fish on two occasions gave Steffi opportunities to see for herself what was *inside* a fish. Margaret went on to cook the fish and at lunch, Steffi could see and taste (if she wished) how the inside had transformed through the process of being cooked.

The book afforded Steffi the chance to talk about some things she knew about and probably to extend her knowledge about animals that live underground. Jackie was a keen gardener, so from when Steffi was quite young, she was out in the garden with her mum, picking up bugs and finding out about them.

Two more cooking sessions

By the time she was four years, six months, Steffi was becoming adept at cooking.

BAKING BISCUITS

An account from Steffi's Family Worker. Steffi, Dana, Cara and Hamish sat down together when they knew we were going to bake today. I read through the recipe and Steffi asked to crack the eggs. She waited for others in the group to complete their part of the process. There was lots of interested chat about what each other was doing. Steffi really enjoyed cracking open and whisking the eggs and then adding them to the mixture. All the children rolled the mixture into small balls. Steffi made 'lots of little biscuits and a great big one'. When they came out of the oven, Steffi commented that they had 'changed colour'.

MAKING PIZZA

Steffi enjoyed the whole process of making pizza from the mixing of the dough, following instructions on the pack and measuring the required amount of water to kneading and rolling out her dough, then leaving it to rise and finally decorating her pizza, which was very symmetrical and which she took a long time over. Steffi reflected later, 'putting the cheese on and mushrooms and pepper'.

Analysis and discussion

Cracking open eggs to reveal what was *inside* probably gave Steffi immense pleasure. She knew what was *contained* inside each egg and it took some skill to crack it and to separate the parts, that had previously been a whole. She was also part of a team who were co-operating together to make biscuits, a transformation of the ingredients when put together. She chose to be creative and to make 'lots of little biscuits and a great big one' reflecting her interest in size *seriation*. She noticed and commented on the 'transformation' in colour when the biscuits came out of the oven.

Drawing and writing using symbols

Steffi's sister, Brogan, was only two years older than her and had attended nursery just before Steffi started and was now at primary school. This may have influenced some of Steffi's mark making play.

'It's for Daddy'

At three years, ten months, Steffi was making some marks on paper and said 'It's for Daddy ...'. Hamish asked her what it said. 'Ex and oh and tee'.

Analysis and discussion

We can deduce from this that Steffi knew that marks were a form of communication. She was making marks to give to her daddy. Objects and notes were often *transported* from home to nursery and back again by children *connecting* their actions and interests in one place to another. She also seemed to know that each mark had a corresponding sound that, in schema terms, mirrored *intersection*, *enclosure* and *intersection* respectively.

Drawing dinosaurs

Two days later, Steffi drew the three dinosaur pictures as shown in Figure 5.6.

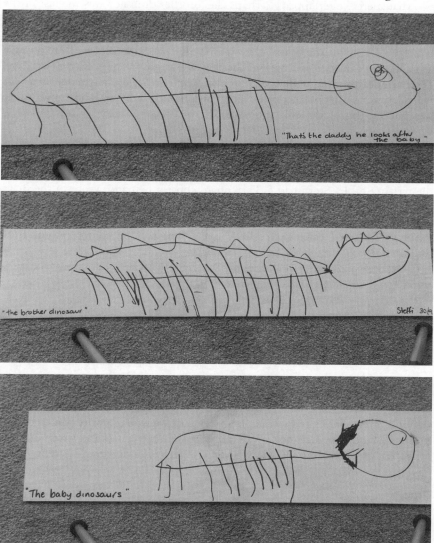

Figure 5.6 Steffi's dinosaur drawings: (a) daddy, (b) brother and (c) baby.

Analysis and discussion

Here Steffi combined *enclosures* with *lines* for each body. She *connected* another smaller *enclosure* for the heads and *contained* inside the head space was the eye. The *connection* between head and body had received some attention. What is not recorded is the order in which she drew these three drawings. The 'brother dinosaur' has a much better connection between head and body than the other two that merely overlapped. Perhaps the 'brother dinosaur' was the last of the three. Also, there's the suggestion of a 'mouth' on each drawing but the 'brother dinosaur' has an open mouth, which, again may have been a third attempt. Although the 'form' of each is similar, she differentiated by doing a wavy line on the head and back of the brother, almost a suggestion of a *zigzag*. The baby seems more wide eyed and also to have a lot of hair in one area.

In connection to Steffi's other great interest in families, she stated quite clearly that 'the daddy looks after the baby'.

Using the writing area

Two weeks later, at three years, eleven months, Steffi and her friend were at the writing table. Steffi had a diary open, chose a pen and wrote in the diary and carefully made four symbols between the lines – two symbols similar to + or x and o or T (Figure 5.7).

She then ripped a sheet of pad and five symbols on it, saying 'nuh oh nuh' (Figure 5.8).

Later, Steffi and Dana were drawing when Steffi says it's her family and adds 'you need it to get to Disneyland'.

Analysis and discussion

Steffi's writing revealed a lot about her knowledge at that time. She knew that you wrote individual letters that had corresponding sounds. She also knew that you had to write things down in order to 'go to Disneyland', so going to Disneyland was functionally dependent on writing something. This may have been your name. It probably was not a coincidence that she produced five symbols and there were five people in her family, who possibly wanted to go to Disneyland. She had not quite worked out that a name is made up of a collection of letters but she was well on the way to understanding that.

Drawing a dragon

One of Steffi's favourite stories was 'On the Way Home'. At four years, three days she drew the dragon from that story (Figure 5.9).

WEEK 3

Steffi   14·10·03

15/3

JANUARY

15

Tuesday

M		7	14	21	:
T	1	8	15	22	:
W	2	9	16	23	:
T	3	10	17	24	:
F	4	11	18	25	
S	5	12	19	26	
S	6	13	20	27	

8.00

8.30

9.00

9.30

10.00

10.30

11.00

11.30

12.00

12.30

Lunch

1.00

1.30

2.00

2.30

3.00

3.30

4.00

4.30

5.00

5.30

Evening Appointments

Figure 5.7 One of Steffi's early attempts at writing.

Steffi   14.10

ʃ † × ⊐ ⊘

" nuh oh nuh "

Figure 5.8 More early writing.

"On the way Home
   ... It's the dragon"
(a favourite story)
                Steffi. 17/11

Figure 5.9 Steffi's dragon drawing.

Analysis and discussion

Here we see two developments in Steffi's mark making: first, the eyes have become a little more refined with *dabs* or *enclosures* inside *enclosures* and, second, Steffi has used *zigzags* (or 'open continuous triangles' Athey 1990: 106) to represent the dragon's back, the little girl's teeth, the tail and possibly hair or fire on the dragon's head. Even the girl's arm looks as though it is bent at the elbow, using the *zigzag* form.

Developing her drawing and storying

Often Steffi was both drawing and making up stories. She drew the Figure 5.10 at four years, three months and said 'This is the big daddy penguin – he lives in the snow … he comes down the snow to look at a snake' (Figure 5.10).

Steffi .
02/04

"This is the big
daddy penguin –
he lives in the snow
… he comes down
the snow to look at
a snake "

Figure 5.10 Steffi's drawing for her penguin story.

Analysis and discussion

Steffi had continued to practise and refine her use of *enclosures* and *zigzags*. Her representation of snow seemed to also be about difference in size as she drew three big balls and three small balls, making a *one to one correspondence* each time. She drew this in February so maybe there had been a smattering of snow and she had been making snowballs. Her *zigzags* had become much bolder and the *connections* to the main *enclosure* a lot neater than they were when she drew the three dinosaurs.

Making a link

Steffi (aged four years, three months) chose the 'Rainbow Fish'. She traced over the letters and said 'Does that say Rainbow Fish?'. I said 'Yes' and she smiled, pleased with herself.

Analysis and discussion

This observation demonstrates that Steffi was generalising some of her learning about the correspondence between marks and meaning. She was checking that the symbols on the front of the book matched the title of the story that she knew well. She was now drawing deductions based on information she had already, a kind of 'problem solving' approach to reading, which would stand her in good stead and also build her confidence about reading and working things out for herself.

Looking at an alphabet book

A week later, Steffi asked to have a 'Dinosaur ABC Book' read at grouptime. She was really interested that 'S' was for Stephanie and 'S' was for Stegosaurus. She asked me 'What begins with Holly?' and we looked it up.

Analysis and discussion

Here Steffi seemed to accommodate to how the symbolic system worked by matching and noticing what began with the same letter as her own name. Then she wanted to know what began with the letter her sister Holly's name began with. Again, she was deducing that if one of the dinosaur names began with the first letter of her name, then another dinosaur name would begin with the first letter of her sister's name. This was a sort of 'working theory' that she was beginning to test out.

Learning about families and being strong

An interest that seemed to endure and to be apparent in all of Steffi's play, was her interest in families, including animal families, and in 'being strong'. Steffi's mum reported that for a long time, Steffi wanted to be a boy. We thought that was because she thought boys were stronger.

Making up stories

When Steffi was aged four years, one month, her Family Worker wrote:

> Steffi regularly asks for the basket of puppets and we make up stories about them or re-enact stories like *Red Riding Hood* or *The Three Little Pigs*. Steffi likes to make up stories about animals getting killed by other fierce animals.

Analysis and discussion

Steffi seemed to want to understand about the transformation between alive and dead. Athey (1990: 201) pointed out that some 'transformations' are 'difficult to anticipate in the mind' and probably none more than alive and dead for a young child. Using the puppets and making up stories was a way of exploring her ideas in a safe way and also of making things happen in her play that she wanted to talk about.

'Fergus the Farm Dog' story sack

Around the same time, Margaret wrote:

> I gathered together a story sack for the story 'Fergus the Farm Dog'. It included the animals and jigsaw puzzles featuring farm animals and their young. Steffi played with the story sack for over an hour – she was interested that baby animals could have different names from their mums and dads, for example 'goats and kids'.

Analysis and discussion

Steffi's working theory seemed to be that animals are *classified* or grouped into types with the same name. Through this play and her conversation with Margaret, she seemed to accommodate to the idea that there is another finer *classification* between adults and baby animals, whereby the groups can have different name labels. We saw from other observations that Steffi was interested in *size seriation*. This information also may have contributed to her understanding of recognising who were the bigger (and maybe stronger) animals and which were the smaller, younger and weaker animals from their names. So, Steffi was discovering what kind of information can be contained in a name, which is a symbol.

Being a dog

'I was being a naughty dog – Courtney was taking me for a walk but he be'd naughty and ran off without anybody … and he found a new family'.

Analysis and discussion

Within the story, Steffi seemed to re-enact one of those early *trajectory* journeys, whereby the fear is that we'll get lost and be alone. However, her anxiety is appeased when she, as the naughty dog, finds a new family. The 'form' the story takes (her story*line*) is recognisable throughout the world and logical and already, Steffi had developed a believable storyline with a climax and resolution.

Within the language she used, we can also see that she had gained some generalisable rules about grammar and the past tense. Correct grammar could be either 'he was naughty' or 'he had been naughty'. What Steffi adopted was a general rule of adding the suffix 'ed' that can be applied to many verbs to make them past tense but not to 'to be'. So Steffi was now demonstrating some of the generalisations she had made and also her current working theories about them. Later on, she would accommodate to the idea that there are many exceptions in English to the past tense rule.

Playing with transformation symbolically

After Christmas, Margaret wrote:

> At grouptime, we went to the soft room. Steffi asked if we could play at 'Aslan'. She was Aslan – I was Peter or Lucy turned to stone and she would look and point at me and I would come back to life.

Analysis and discussion

Here Steffi was using and trying out what she knew from *The Lion, the Witch and the Wardrobe* to explore a bit more about transformation, this time from being 'turned to stone' to 'coming back to life'.

What happened over Christmas?

Steffi was chatting to Margaret and her Family Group about what had happened over Christmas, when she had not come to nursery. 'Steffi told us that she went to the cinema to see *Nemo* and also that her pet mouse had died "cos she was sixteen".'

Analysis and discussion

There was a striking similarity in 'form' between the 'Nemo' story and some of the themes of lost and found that Steffi was exploring in the stories she created.

Also her pet mouse had died. Death was another concept Steffi was interested in. The explanation she had been given and accepted was that 'she was sixteen'. I am sure that went along with an explanation that that was very, very old, for a mouse (according to Wikipedia, mice usually live between one and three years so sixteen may have been what Steffi considered a large number). Conceptually, what Steffi was forming was a sense of the difference in life span between different creatures and also of acceptance that, if someone was old for their species, it was time to die or their journey had come to an end and this was okay.

Playing with transformation in her thinking

At four years, two months, Steffi told Margaret: 'My mum's going to swim with the dolphins when she's a mermaid'.

Analysis and discussion

Here we can see that Steffi was playing with this idea of transformation. Her mum may have said that she wanted to swim with the dolphins. In her head, Steffi changed (or could imagine) her mum, as a mermaid, and, therefore, able to swim with the dolphins.

Being strong

Steffi (four years, two months) was wonderfully animated and made loud 'pterodactyl' noises as she flapped it across the room then banged it several times on the cabinet.

Analysis and discussion

Here Steffi was using a figure to represent strength and power (Figure 5.11). She articulated this by being loud and using the figure to make a noise by banging it on the cabinet. In terms of schemas, she made a journey with the dinosaur figure across the room (a *trajectory*), then banged it in an up/down movement (*trajectory*) while simultaneously using sound *seriation* to signify or symbolise strength.

Figure 5.11 Steffi and her pterodactyl.

A story for Margaret

A few weeks later (at four years, three months)

> On the minibus on the way to Kid's Kingdom, Steffi made up a story for me:

'When I was four, a big dragon came and ate you up and a fairy came to look after me and my magic pony, but my horse is dead now.' Later Steffi added, 'When my mummy's granny died, my horse died'.

Analysis and discussion

Steffi seemed to be playing with ideas about loss and rescue, but also trying to understand why her horse died when her mum's granny died. Maybe she was thinking 'What if a dragon came and ate up Margaret?' In her story, a fairy appeared, who looked after her and her magic pony. Her final remark seemed to be an afterthought. Perhaps she was searching for a connection between two deaths.

Feeling strong

The next day, Steffi was engaged in chasing games most of the morning alongside Stephen, John, Daniel, Karim and Tanya. Fantasy themes included:

- lost dogs
- Goldilocks
- Aslan
- finding the wolf who killed our mum and dad
- venom marks/poisonous snakes
- lots of dying/coming back to life
- running fast/climbing high to get away.

Analysis and discussion

This was a new development, for Steffi to play with a group of children, mostly boys. She may have been testing out some of her theories about strength related to gender. The themes explored offer some insights into the related concepts: being lost and found; death and dying; how you die; whether you can come back to life; escape. In schema terms, there was lots of running and chasing (*trajectory*), escaping seemed to be functionally dependent on running fast or climbing high (both *trajectories* concerned with the concepts of speed and height).

On a visit to the zoo

That same month, when Steffi was four years, three months, her group went on a visit to the zoo. Margaret reported that, 'Steffi was delighted to spot the elephants before I did. She named them mummy, daddy and baby. Steffi did the most amazing spontaneous roar when the lion did'.

Analysis and discussion

Here Steffi was applying her seriation schema to the elephants by naming them mummy, daddy and baby, which in her mind might have meant strongest (usually 'daddy'), strong (usually 'mummy') and least strong (usually 'baby').

Steffi seemed to act as though she knew the lion and was his 'soul mate'. In her mind, he was probably 'Aslan' although she did not verbalise this. For her Aslan (and therefore the lion) was associated with supreme strength and power.

Conclusion

In this chapter we have seen how well Steffi's interests were supported both at home and at nursery. She was particularly close to Katey (co-author of this chapter and Deputy Head of Centre) and to Margaret (her Family Worker). Both seemed to be able to tune in to both the 'content' and 'form' that was of interest to Steffi.

Steffi needed long periods of uninterrupted play in order to explore some emerging concepts such as 'lost and found', 'danger and rescue' and 'life and death'. Everything she chose to explore was acceptable in both environments. The themes explored came from her.

We saw Steffi become stronger through trying out being strong in her play. She tested out many of her theories and sometimes accommodated new learning.

Reflections and questions

- We believe that we are trying to 'uncover' the curriculum in each child – what thoughts do you have about what we provided to extend Steffi's learning, for example, 'gutting fish'?
- Steffi seemed to be developing lots of ideas about writing and reading. How could we foster those ideas and help her understand conventional symbols?
- Steffi often played with adults. How influenced do you think children are, by their play partners?

Steffi's interests now

Figure 5.12 Steffi now.

Steffi is eleven years old (Figure 5.12). She remembers being at nursery when Katey (worker) was with her in the sand. Steffi made a hole in the sand and told Katey she was building a lion's nest. Steffi likes drawing, animals and dinosaurs. She also said that 'although it sounds a bit weird for an eleven-year-old', she likes just running about. When she grows up, she wants to be a vet or a doctor. Steffi doesn't like pumpkins. She explained that she was at her mum's friend's house, making pumpkin soup when it exploded. Steffi also added that she doesn't like ghosts or the dark.

Chapter 6

Schemas and links with emotions

Colette Tait

What is Ethan investigating through his schematic explorations?

When we were conceptualising this book, we thought it might be interesting for one of the chapters to focus on a younger child, not yet attending the Pen Green Nursery, but attending another service at the Centre. Therefore, this chapter is in two sections, and focuses on a little boy, Ethan. In the first section of the chapter, Ethan is two years and four months old. The author follows Ethan's schematic explorations over several weeks whilst he attends a parent and child group at Pen Green, called Growing Together. The second section of the chapter revisits Ethan more than a year later, once he has started attending the Pen Green Nursery. He is then three years and five months old.

Ethan's context

Ethan was born on 17 June in 2002. He lives with his mum, Heidi, his dad, Myke, and his little sister, Leah, who is currently seventeen and a half months old. Ethan also had an older sister, Chloe. Chloe attended the Pen Green Nursery but, tragically, died in a car accident when she was three years and eight months old. Chloe would be thirteen years old if she were still alive today. Chloe's memory is still very much alive, and she is often spoken about, both at home at the Centre.

Ethan has several important adults and children in his life. Ethan spends a lot of time with his maternal Grandma and Granddad who 'play with him non-stop'. He sees them regularly, two or three times each week, and often 'stays over' at their house on a Friday night.

He is also close to two family friends, Nicky (Molly's mother) and Molly. Molly is a similar age to Ethan. 'Up until Molly went to pre-school we would spend time with Nicky and Molly five days a week'.

Both Heidi and Myke describe Ethan as "very loving ... as well as being ... very mischievous".

Family involvement at the Pen Green Centre

Heidi originally started attending Pen Green when her eldest daughter, Chloe, was a young baby. She attended the baby massage sessions, a group called 'first steps', and a messy play session with Chloe. Chloe then attended the Pen Green Nursery. After Chloe died, Heidi continued to come to the Centre. She said, 'I did the library in the nursery ... I needed to be there for a while, and then I couldn't be there'.

During this period when Heidi was not coming to the centre, she and Myke moved house. Heidi then found out she was pregnant with Ethan, but not until she 'was nineteen weeks'. Both Heidi and Myke described feeling both 'happy and really, really apprehensive'.

Heidi then began attending groups at Pen Green once again. She attended Great Expectations, a support group for women to attend during their pregnancy. Once Ethan was born, Heidi went to a Breast Feeding Support Group, Baby Massage and Growing Together. So, as Heidi pointed out, Ethan has known the Centre since he was born, and is very familiar with everything. Myke said, it is 'almost home from home'.

Growing Together

At Pen Green we currently run three Growing Together sessions each week. These sessions are run as drop-in groups for parents with children aged up to three years of age. The groups are well staffed by workers with different backgrounds and skills, who are 'able to get to know families well, and provide a regular, reliable and supportive service' (Pen Green Research Base 2004).

The following Child Development and Psychoanalytic concepts underpin the work in Growing Together:

- involvement (Laevers 1997)
- well-being (Laevers 1997)
- schemas (Athey 1990)
- pedagogic strategies (Whalley and Arnold 1997)
- holding (Winnicott 1965)
- containment (Bion 1962)
- attachment (Bowlby 1969).

We have found it very useful to share these underpinning concepts with parents, in a similar way to that in which Chris Athey shared schematic theory with parents in the Froebel Nursery Project (1973–1978).

The Growing Together groups have a series of aims, to:

- give parents a chance to play with their child in a stimulating and secure environment;

- help parents to understand more about their relationship with their child;
- have dialogue with parents about their child's development;
- encourage reflective parenting (through reflecting on video material filmed in the sessions);
- facilitate parent to parent support;
- validate the feelings women are experiencing when they are suffering from postnatal depression;
- encourage helpful attachment experiences through video feedback and discussions.

Ethan, attended one of the Growing Together groups with his sister, Leah, and his mum, Heidi.

Ethan and his family

Ethan appears to be very close to Heidi, Myke and Leah. Myke works a constant 6.00 AM to 2.00 PM shift as a crane driver in a warehouse, locally. Usually, Heidi cares for the children the majority of the time during the day. However, as Heidi returned to work, in the evenings, when Ethan was twenty weeks old, Myke has always put Ethan to bed, and still does. They have a routine where Ethan, as soon as he goes upstairs, dives under his quilt. He then has a wash, 'with his own soap', gets into bed and lies with his dad for 'a chat and a cuddle' before he goes to sleep.

Heidi commented that it is really nice to see Ethan with Leah, 'he loves her to death, he's brilliant with her'. She reported that, 'you can step out of the room and peep – he'll check she's okay and give her different toys to play with'.

Section 1: Ethan at Growing Together

Ethan's interests

Ethan spent a lot of time both at Growing Together and at home playing with train sets. Heidi reported that Ethan, at two years and four months old, loved watching *Thomas the Tank Engine* videos, and playing with his 'Thomas' crane. He had enjoyed watching the video and seeing the crane being used to pick 'Thomas' up when he was derailed! During the observation period, Heidi and her dad took Ethan on a trip to see Thomas the Tank Engine at Lamport, a village nearby. Ethan was able to have the first-hand experience of travelling on a train. After the visit to see Thomas, Ethan played with the idea that he could name himself after one of the Thomas the Tank Engine characters. Heidi called Leah 'Leah Jayne'. Ethan said to Heidi, 'Ethan Jayne?' Heidi replied, 'No, Ethan Michael'. Ethan retorted, 'No, Ethan Gordon', after the engine named Gordon.

Ethan also loved to build tall towers with his Duplo. He would build so high that Myke had to pick Ethan up to put more bricks on top of his tower. Heidi reported that whenever Ethan went to his granddad's he would spend a lot of time shovelling hard core from one area in the garden to another. When I observed Ethan at the drop-in, he spent time shovelling sand into a wheelbarrow and wheeling it around the beach area before depositing it elsewhere.

Selecting the video material for analysis

I decided to analyse video footage of Ethan playing with the train set at Growing Together as he returned to it week after week. It seemed to be important to him. The analysis is of video material gathered on three different days.

Throughout the three sequences Ethan was playing with the train on the train track (Figure 6.1). The train was connected together with magnets. He spent time connecting the train together and moving it around the track. He moved the train forwards and backwards and over the hump-backed bridge again and again. He watched closely the motion of the train as it travelled over the track. He moved an engine around the track without making contact with it, but by utilising the opposing magnetic forces, usually used to connect the train carriages together.

Figure 6.1 Ethan with a train set.

Analysis and discussion: Ethan's schemas

It became evident almost immediately that Ethan had a cluster of schemas which included *trajectory, transporting, connecting, containing, enveloping, rotation* and *going through a boundary*.

When I spent time with Heidi and Myke they reported a vast amount of *trajectory* behaviour which included an interest in *lines*. Ethan spent time lining up objects, such as his Bob the Builder toys. He lined these toys up in front of the door, side by side. When Ethan and his family were at Butlins he enjoyed parking all the 'Little Tykes Coupes' in a line. Mike pointed out that 'The line has to be perfect'. He spends time building with his Duplo bricks, building high towers. The line is the figurative aspect of the trajectory. 'The trajectory is the forerunner of higher-order notions, such as distance, length and speed' (Athey 1990: 138).

Ethan's interest in the 'Thomas' crane revealed a coordination of schemas – *trajectory* and *rotation*. The length of the rope on the crane is functionally dependent on the rotation of the handle. As Ethan turned the handle one way the rope became longer, and as he turned the handle in the opposite direction the rope became shorter, so lifting the train up.

Heidi and Myke also spoke about Ethan's love of 'transporting', 'carrying objects or being carried from one place to another' (Arnold 1999: 22). Athey states,

> When a 2 year old establishes starting-points and points of arrival during transporting behaviour he or she is presumed, by Piaget, to be experiencing physically early equivalence of distance, length and speed by traversing A to B on a horizontal plane and then B to A on the same plane
>
> (1990: 136)

I think that distance, length and speed are the concepts that Ethan is exploring in his play with the train set, and on the beach (Figure 6.2).

A new interest?

Heidi said that for about 'the last three weeks' she had noticed that Ethan had been *enveloping* things. On the home video that Myke filmed, Ethan spent time hiding his Duplo bricks under a blanket, saying 'Where all the bricks gone? ... Bricks gone night nights ... Bricks hiding'. Here Ethan was using his *envelopment* schema in a symbolic way as he was pretending that bricks go to bed and can hide! Athey says that 'Exploration of envelopment comes later than the exploration of trajectories' (1990: 149). In the second section of this chapter Ethan's *envelopment* schema became much more evident.

Figure 6.2 Ethan using sand to envelop on the beach.

Analysis of the video extract

In the first part of the video Ethan had four carriages joined together, and he was pulling the train around the track and back again. At home, Heidi reported that Ethan liked to make his train as long as he could, using all the carriages they have. Ethan was experimenting; each time that he added a carriage to his train it became longer, and each time he took one away it became shorter. Arnold reports that in a similar way Harry 'connects trains and carriages together to increase the length' (Arnold 2003: 102). Athey says that 'When number as discrete elements can be combined or partitioned in order to vary length, the teacher is in business for the development of linear measurement' (1990: 190). Ethan was gaining understanding about linear measurement through using the train set. As Ethan moved the train around the track the length of the train remained the same, but looked different when it was on a straight piece of track, in comparison to when it was on a bend. Perceptually the line appeared shorter, however conceptually the length was identical.

Ethan also spent time pulling the train to the top of the hump-backed bridge and then letting go and watching the train move back down the bridge. In terms of physics when Ethan did this again and again, he was exploring 'Momentum – the quantity of motion of a moving body' (*Concise Oxford English Dictionary* 1990: 764) (Figure 6.3).

Figure 6.3 Ethan experimenting with momentum.

At one point on the video as Ethan was moving the train backwards he verbalised 'Backwards'. Heidi replied, 'Going backwards are you?' Vygotsky says that 'word calls to mind its content … every word is a generalisation or a concept' (1986: 212). In this instance the 'content' was the train and the 'form' (or emerging concept) was 'backwards'. As Ethan was able to verbalise 'backwards' when he was actually making the train travel backwards then we can assume he had a sound understanding of the concept of 'backwards'. Heidi has also reported that Ethan had spent a lot of time sitting on his Little Tykes Transporter, at home, and making it travel backwards.

Sometimes Ethan was moving the train quite fast, and the engine and carriages separated when he was moving the train over the bridge. Heidi said that Ethan knew you have to go slower if you want the train to remain intact. There is evidence of this on the video, where Ethan was moving the train quickly, and then he slowly pulled the train over the bridge. In this instance the train remaining *connected* together was functionally dependent on the speed with which Ethan propelled it over the bridge.

In the second sequence, Ethan's train was much longer. Heidi asked him, 'Is it a long train?' Ethan replied in a disappointed tone, 'No'. He then pointed to an engine and said 'That one'. Heidi told him that it 'won't stick to that one'. Ethan had made his train with an engine at the front and six carriages behind it. The only remaining pieces of train were engines. The train set had been designed so that the engines must go at the front of the train. Ethan was unable to join the engine to the back of his line of carriages as the magnets that connect the train together repel each other. Ethan then spent time moving his train behind the spare engine, thus propelling it around the track. Heidi verbalised, 'It's pushing it away isn't it?' Ethan smiled, he seemed pleased with himself.

Ethan continued to propel the engine around the track using the magnetic force. He then removed his existing engine and replaced it with the one he had propelled around the track. He appeared to be very pleased with himself. He was 'chuffed' (Tait 2004).

In the final sequence, Ethan spent time connecting his train together. At one point he had used all the carriages. He turned to reach for an engine, and then didn't pick it up (Figure 6.4). Had Ethan 'accommodated' (Athey 1990: 38) the new learning – that the engine would not attach itself to the back of his line of carriages because of the magnetic forces?

Figure 6.4 Ethan reaching for the engine, and not selecting it, but returning to his play.

Section 2: Ethan at Pen Green Nursery

Ethan left the Growing Together group when he became three and I knew that he had begun attending the nursery. I wondered how Ethan had settled into the nursery? I wondered if he was playing in a similar way to that which I had observed a year earlier? I wanted to observe Ethan and try to find out 'What's going on inside ... his ... head?' (Soale 2004). Would Ethan be carrying out similar investigations to those that he was carrying out when he attended Growing Together?

Each observation is illustrated in turn, with the analysis for each observation immediately after it.

Observation 1: Ethan and the taps

In this first sequence of three pictures (Figure 6.5) you can see Ethan using a paper towel which he has held under the tap to make wet. He then held the paper towel by two corners and pressed it against the mirror, thus hiding his reflection. He looked towards me; I was filming. Ethan then took the paper towel off the mirror and looked at his reflection (Figure 6.6).

Next Ethan covered the tap with wet paper towels (Figure 6.7). He layered one paper towel on top of another, repeatedly. He then bent down, as if to see if he could still see the tap he had just covered.

Ethan then put his hand under the paper towels, as if to feel if the tap was still there. He then placed a dry paper towel on top of the other paper towels, and looked to me and pointed to the tap saying, 'where's the tap gone?'

Ethan covered the second tap with another dry paper towel. There were many paper towels layered on top of each other, *enveloping* the taps. He put another couple of paper towels on for good measure and looked towards me with an expression of chuffedness (Tait 2004), as though he was extremely pleased with himself. He said that 'two taps are gone'. I responded by laughing and saying, 'two taps *are* gone'.

Analysis of observations

It is evident from these video observations and from other data gathered that Ethan was exploring a cluster of schemas. Ethan's cluster of schemas included: *trajectory*, *transporting*, *containing*, *enveloping*, *connecting* and *going through a boundary*. Ethan exhibited the same cluster of schemas as identified a year ago in Growing Together, with the exception of 'rotation'. A year ago, rotation featured quite obviously in Ethan's play, but in these observations there was no evidence of rotation.

Figure 6.5 Ethan playing with a wet paper towel and a mirror.

Figure 6.6 Ethan continues his play with the towel and mirror.

Figure 6.7 Ethan hides the tap.

Analysis of Observation 1: Ethan and the taps

In this sequence Ethan was primarily using his *envelopment* schema to cover over things, first his own reflection in the mirror, and then the taps. At home, Heidi and Myke reported that Ethan hid under his quilt, saying to them, 'I'm gonna run and hide under my quilt and you won't be able to find me'. Ethan also liked to hide objects and ask Myke to find them. However, if Myke asked him where the object was, Ethan always told him.

As Ethan put the paper towel onto the mirror his reflection disappeared, and as he removed the paper towel his reflection reappeared. I asked Ethan, as I was filming him, whether he thought the paper towel would stick to the mirror if he let go. He took no notice of me. Heidi reported, however, that he would understand that the paper towel would stick if it was wet. We can therefore make the assumption that Ethan appeared to understand that 'wetness in some objects can act as an adhesive' (Athey 2005).

Shaw (1991: 288) found, in her study, that 'parents' interpretations at times appeared more accurate than the researcher's interpretations. Throughout this research process I often found myself 'checking things out' with Heidi or Myke who were able to either refute or confirm my thoughts and hypotheses about Ethan.

In the sequence where Ethan covered the taps, he was in control of making the taps disappear. Heidi and Myke reported that when Ethan was at home he often played games in which he had all the control. He asked Heidi and Myke, for instance, which train would move first, when he had set up several trains. Whichever train Heidi or Myke selected was wrong. Heidi wondered 'does he know he's in control of the outcome?' Myke commented, 'He dictates how we play it'. Dahlberg *et al.* (1999: 50) state that 'the young child should be taken seriously. Active and competent, he or she has ideas and theories that are not only worth listening to, but also merit scrutiny and, where appropriate, questioning and challenge'. By entering into Ethan's games in this way Heidi and Myke were taking Ethan seriously, as well as questioning and challenging him.

Ethan understood that the apparent disappearance of the taps was functionally dependent on him covering them with the paper towels. I wonder whether when Ethan was bending down to look under the paper towels, and when he put his finger under the taps if he was really making sure that they were out of sight for other people?

I think that Ethan was playful in this sequence. After he had *enveloped* one tap, he asked me 'where's the tap gone', and then at the end, after *enveloping* both taps, Ethan stated, 'two taps gone', and looked to me for a reaction. Athey states that when the child knows something so well 'he or she can even play with it' (1990: 38). From this we can therefore assume that Ethan knew that the taps were still there, he understood about object permanence, but that he was playing with the notion of them not being there.

Observation 2: Ethan and the buggy

In Figure 6.8 we can see Ethan pushing the buggy. He had put sand into the base of the buggy to cover it (*envelopment*). Although the sand was *contained* in the buggy, it seemed important to Ethan that he spread it out across the base of the buggy, thus *enveloping* it. He had then gone to the tap and filled the buggy with water. The water seeped out of the joints in the buggy. Ethan told me 'water's coming out'. I asked if the sand would also come out. He told me 'No'. Ethan was holding the buggy still, and allowing the water to settle. He then experimented with moving the buggy backwards and forwards a small amount, causing the water to flow back and forth inside the buggy. He then strode off purposefully.

Figure 6.8 Ethan pushing the buggy.

Ethan gained speed and crashed into the buggy, so displacing a volume of water. I commented that a lot of water went out of the front of the buggy and a small amount came out of the back of the buggy. Ethan returned to the tap to repeat his experiment. Ethan did this again and again, crashing into different objects, and watching what happened to the displaced water.

Analysis of Observation 2: Ethan and the buggy

In this sequence, Ethan was primarily using his *trajectory, transporting* and *containing* schemas to displace volumes of water. However, at the beginning Ethan had *enveloped* the bottom of the buggy with sand, before filling it with water. He already understood that the wooden buggy would allow water to seep through its joints, but wouldn't allow the sand to 'disappear'.

After Ethan had filled the buggy with water for the first time he told me it was very heavy as he moved it backwards slowly. Athey (2005) states, 'he started to transport the water backwards with great caution but acquired confidence with competence'. When he said 'it's very heavy' Athey (op. cit.) states that 'he is accounting for the instability of the water by weight'. I feel that Ethan understood that the motion of the water inside the buggy was functionally dependent upon the speed with which he moved the buggy. Through his transporting behaviour, Ethan was experiencing physically 'equivalence of distance, length and speed by traversing A to B on a horizontal plane and the B to A on the same plane' (Athey 1990: 136), but with 'deliberately added complications' (Athey 2005).

When Ethan 'crashed' the wooden buggy into the other buggy, and subsequently other objects, he caused a volume of water to be displaced. Physics is the science of 'dealing with the properties and interactions of matter and energy' (*Concise Oxford English Dictionary* 1990: 897). In physics terms, Ethan may have been exploring 'Momentum – the quantity of motion of a moving body' (*Concise Oxford English Dictionary* 1990: 764). In the first section of this chapter, just over a year earlier, I also thought that Ethan was interested in momentum – he was repeatedly pulling a train to the top of a hump-backed bridge and then letting go and watching the train move back down the bridge. However, this play with the buggy and water seemed more complex. In this instance the amount of water displaced was dependent on the speed at which Ethan approached the object, the solidity of the object and the force of the impact.

Ethan was also experimenting with forces and impact at home. He was experimenting with crashing himself into different materials. Heidi reported that he liked to crash into piles of leaves on his scooter and into the hedge. She said he was interested in the end result, 'he does it in so many ways ... there has to be a different impact'. Whilst I was at Ethan's house, he spent a lot of time crashing his trains into each other, and derailing them. There was a broken train on a shelf which Ethan pointed out to me. I asked him what had happened and he said, 'I crashed it with my other things'. Therefore Ethan knew that objects can break if too much force is used.

Observation 3: Ethan and the trowel

Ethan dug some mud from a small sand and mud pool. He then tipped it into the sand and went to wash his dirty trowel.

As Ethan moved his trowel nearer to the tap the water splashed up and hit him in the face Ethan seemed to be shocked. This didn't appear to be what he was expecting. Ethan then moved the trowel up in the flow of water again, but this time leaned back so that he didn't get splashed.

As he held the trowel in the flow of water my boots got wet. I asked Ethan if he was trying to wet my boots. He smiled, and held the trowel slightly differently, thus altering the flow of water to avoid wetting my boots.

Ethan repeated similar actions for more than twenty minutes. He held the trowel at different angles, and different heights in the water to see the effect. He commented on the water reaching the bush.

Ethan asked me to remove the hose attachment which was on the tap. Ethan then repeated his experiment. I asked if the water splashed differently without the attachment. Ethan turned to me and told me it was noisier. It was. Ethan pointed to the mud which he put into the sand and said 'where's the mud going?' I commented that it was underneath the water, and that the water was making a big puddle. Ethan then fetched another trowel and said, 'I'm going to try this one'. I told him that it was a good idea.

Analysis of Observation 3: Ethan and the trowel

This observation was also to do with displacement of water, but through the use of a trowel against the moving flow of water from the tap. The direction the displaced water went in was functionally dependent on the position in which Ethan placed the trowel. Athey (2005) states that Ethan 'can vary his end point – bush rather than boots. Direction and distance'. We know that Ethan understood this as he changed the direction of the water when I said that my boots were getting wet.

To begin with, the water splashed Ethan's face. His look of surprise made me think that he wasn't expecting that to happen. He became 'disequilibrated' (Spencer Pulaski 1971: 56). Ethan 'accommodated' (Athey 1990) this new piece of information, and the next time he put the trowel into the flow of water he leaned backwards, so as not to get wet.

Throughout this sequence Ethan was continuously experimenting, and assimilating new content 'into developing cognitive structures' (Athey 1990: 33). He carried out the same action with two different trowels, but with varying pressures of water – by turning the tap on and off, and by asking me to remove the hose attachment.

Through pushing the trowel against the vertical trajectory of water, Ethan transformed the *vertical trajectory* into lots of *horizontal trajectories*, in a *core and radial* configuration. Interestingly, when I was visiting Ethan at home he said that he was going to 'crash' his train set. On four occasions he pulled a long train, quite quickly, and 'crashed' it by turning the front engine to a right angle, over the barrier for the level crossing. So, he changed a *vertical trajectory* to a *horizontal trajectory*. Was Ethan becoming interested in angles too?

Ethan and his train set at home

Ethan was still very interested in playing with his train set at home. He now had many different types and sizes of trains. These trains all connected together in different ways. Myke says that Ethan 'experiments with what fits together, he tries to mix and match them ... and manages'. Whilst I was visiting Ethan and his family at home I observed Ethan playing with his train set. He was spending time connecting different types of carriage together. He knew immediately that if two magnets did not connect, that he needed to turn one of the carriages around. A year ago, in Growing Together, Ethan was experimenting with this. Now, there was no hesitation. He had accommodated this information and automatically made the adjustments without appearing to think about them.

Ethan was also experimenting with forces in another way. He made a long train from quite large carriages, and connected a small battery-operated engine to the train. The engine pulled the carriages very slowly. As he was turning the engine on Ethan hypothesised, 'It might not pull it'. Ethan was taking into account the size of the engine in comparison to the size and length of the train.

Another thought – is there an emotional connection for Ethan?

Throughout Ethan's investigations at nursery he had demonstrated strong *enveloping* behaviour; a schema which Ethan had just begun to demonstrate over a year ago at home. After we had observed Ethan in Growing Together Heidi reported that for about 'the last three weeks' she had noticed that Ethan had been enveloping things. As Athey states 'Exploration of envelopment comes later than the exploration of trajectories' (1990: 149) it was not surprising that we were seeing much more *envelopment* in Ethan's nursery observations.

In the observations reported above Ethan was enveloping on several different occasions, in different ways. He was:

• Using a paper towel to hide his reflection from himself in the nursery bathroom.

- Layering paper towels over the taps in the bathroom and making them disappear.
- *Enveloping* the base of the buggy with sand, before adding a layer of water on top of the sand.
- He commented on the mud he had thrown into the sandpit which had been *enveloped* by water, but could still be seen.

In addition to these examples of envelopment, throughout this period of observation Ethan was very interested in objects being buried in the large sandpit, known at Pen Green as the 'beach'. He repeatedly asked Margaret, his Family Worker, 'What is at the bottom of the sandpit?' Margaret told Ethan that there was a 'black liner' at the bottom of the sand pit. She dug down to show Ethan. I observed Ethan spotting objects partially buried and excitedly uncovering them.

On one occasion Ethan drew on his *enveloping* schema in his thinking to hypothesise. He showed me a buggy with a wheel missing. When I asked him where it was, he said, 'might be in there, or there, or there' whilst pointing to different areas of the sandpit. He was hypothesising that the missing wheel might be buried somewhere in the beach.

In the analysis so far, I have very much focused on Ethan's cognition. However, I would like to pose a question:

- Is Ethan's *enveloping* schema helping him to come to some sort of understanding about separation and death; people being here and being gone?

Ethan had just started attending the nursery, and so has had to cope with being separated from Heidi, and left in the care of people who he was not as familiar with.

Perhaps through his *enveloping* schema Ethan was playing with the idea that you can be there, but appear to be gone. At home Ethan said, 'I'm gonna run and hide under my quilt and you won't be able to find me'. I wonder how it felt for Ethan to be 'hidden'; to be absent from his parents? In the bathroom at nursery Ethan played with this idea when he *enveloped* the tap with the paper towels and asked me where it has gone.

Perhaps Ethan was playing with the notion that although Heidi leaves him, she will return to collect him. Bowlby states that a three-year-old child, experiencing a short separation 'is less likely to be upset in these situations and is more able to understand that mother will soon return' (1991: 73).

Heidi reported that when she asked Ethan what he had been doing at nursery she got one of two responses. Either he replied 'playing with Callum', or 'Callum wasn't there today'. Again, Ethan seemed interested in here and gone. Either Callum was here and available for Ethan to play with, or he was gone.

Heidi and Myke have pictures of Chloe (Ethan's older sister who died before he was born) up in the living room at home. They speak about Chloe and take Ethan to Chloe's grave 'to do the flowers'. I wonder how Ethan can come to understand that he has two sisters? Leah, who is here all of the time, and Chloe who he has never met, and who is not here now. We knew that Ethan was thinking about Chloe as he had spoken of her in the last two weeks. On one occasion, Heidi and Myke had been sorting things out in the loft. A painted footprint that belonged to Chloe fell to the floor. It was on the floor later when Heidi saw it. She asked Ethan whose the footprint was. Ethan replied, 'Daddy said it was Chloe's'. Although Heidi and Myke have spoken about Chloe, this was the first time that Ethan had made any kind of reference to her.

On another occasion Myke and Ethan were watching the television when Ethan said, '*Boogie Bee Bees* is my programme, *Rubber Dubbers* is Daddy's programme and *Tots TV* was Chloe's favourite ... Chloe's not here now'.

However, how can Ethan think about Chloe, as they have had no shared experiences together on which to draw knowledge? Ethan hasn't had first-hand experience of Chloe (Stern 2005). Bowlby refers to 'the fact that a mother can be physically present but "emotionally" absent' (1991: 43). Perhaps when Heidi and Myke think about Chloe they are temporarily absent in Ethan's mind. Perhaps he was using his *envelopment* schema to think about objects and people being gone temporarily, and permanently.

In order to think about Ethan, I have tried to separate out cognition and emotion. However I agree with Shaw who states, 'there appears to be no dichotomy between feeling and thought in the child's behaviour. Perhaps every act of a child's spontaneous behaviour has an emotional and an intellectual aspect to it' (1991: 344).

Conclusions and thoughts for the future

Spending time closely observing Ethan, and talking with Heidi and Myke on these two occasions has been a thoroughly enjoyable experience, for me. It has brought to light how complex Ethan's development is. Ethan was exploring concepts, such as equivalence of distance, length, speed and momentum, that would not be dealt with in his formal schooling until he is much older. Hopefully, the rich first-hand experiences Ethan was having both at home and in both settings would enable him to gain sound conceptual understanding of the theories he was investigating.

Heidi and Myke have reported that they 'look at Ethan in a different light' as a result of being part of this study. Myke reported that now when Ethan is doing something, that perhaps they would have asked him not to do before, they stand back and think about what he is doing and why.

In terms of the provision at Growing Together, studying Ethan highlighted the need for more extensive provision. We needed more train engines and carriages. There was one occasion when another child wanted to play with the train set too. The child's mother pointed to Ethan's engine and said 'Can I give that to David, as you have one, two, three, four?' as she counted Ethan's carriages. She then proceeded to taken Ethan's engine. Ethan looked at her as though she had no 'common sense'. He just watched, and didn't play with the train again. Heidi commented that he wouldn't play with the carriages alone as he knew it was the engine that made the train go.

We could also have extended Ethan's learning by providing trains that connected together in different ways, so that children could experiment with different types of connectors.

In the nursery Ethan did have access to more resources, such as extensive train track and carriages, together with the beach area and water. Understanding what Ethan was investigating helped staff to plan more effectively for Ethan in the following year.

It may be important for staff and parents to think about the emotional aspect of children's schematic explorations. Certainly some evidence has been gathered to begin to support this argument (Shaw 1991; Arnold 1999, 2003, 2010). This study of Ethan may add to the idea that children are able to use their schemas to work through feelings, and to come to understand abstract concepts.

Reflections and questions

- How could sharing information across a large centre help us to provide for children's and families' needs and interests?
- Ethan seemed very focused on 'doing' and carrying out his own investigations. Could he be missed in a busy environment where the focus is on the curriculum?
- How did Ethan's investigations link with the official curriculum and guidance offered on the curriculum?

Ethan's interests now

Ethan is eight years old (Figure 6.9). He remembers playing with Andrew at nursery and still sees him now. They used to play outside on the bikes. Ethan is good at maths, drawing and PE. He likes balancing on the large equipment. He does not like falling over outside on the playground.

Figure 6.9 Ethan now.

Chapter 7

Schemas and mark making

Kate Hayward

The context

This paper looks at how children's earlier schematic concerns relate to their mark making explorations at home and in school. It is drawn from a small partnership research project, involving children, parents, nursery Family Workers, a researcher and early years practitioners in school. The focus of the research was to look at the relationship between schematic behaviour and the development of mark making.

Five children who had previously attended the Pen Green Nursery were selected for the study. Their nursery Family Workers and their parents reflected on the schemas that they had identified while the children were at nursery and the mark making that had been recorded. The parents, the Foundation Stage 2 practitioners and the researcher made narrative and video observations of the children mark making over a six-week period during the autumn term 2004.

Throughout the project great consideration was given to the ethics of observing and recording children's behaviour in different settings and in particular the use of video. Parents and practitioners gave written consent for their involvement in the project and the reporting of the research findings. The children themselves were asked for their permission for the researcher to observe and video them in school. Two children, John and Caitlin, are the focus of this chapter.

Case study: John, born 15 November 1999

John lives with his younger sister Tishy (three years old at the time of the study), his mother Julie and his father Piers. He attended Pen Green Nursery from September 2002 to July 2004 and started at a local primary school in September 2004 when he was four years, ten months.

John is a very caring boy who always considers others in everything he does. He enjoyed playing with cars and trains and he had a close friendship with Stephen, another of the project children. They would spend periods of time in the nursery constructing the train track and building with the large blocks. John enjoyed physical activity. He had just mastered how to ride a two-wheeled bike at the beginning of the project and at that time he was rarely observed engaging in mark making. He seemed to be very encouraged by the attention to his marks during the project and started making marks at every opportunity. As Julie says, 'At first he didn't make any marks and now he's obsessed with mark making!'

The schemas documented by nursery staff during his time in the nursery were: *trajectory* and *connecting*.

John makes his mark

I showed John (four years, ten months and twenty-eight days) the consent form and explained that I had asked his mum and dad to sign it, to give their permission for me to video and observe John in school. This was our conversation:

Kate: Will you put something here to say that you think it is okay for me to see what you are doing in school and to take your photos and video?

John: Yeah, I'll draw you a strawberry ... Shall I draw you a strawberry?

Kate: That would be great if you can draw me a strawberry to tell me that you think it is okay.

Piers: Why don't you write your name, John? You can write your name for Kate.

John: You can see me write my name at school ... I'll draw you a strawberry. It's red and that's my favourite colour.

(John took a red pen out of the pack and drew an *enclosure* and began to very carefully fill in the shape.)

John: I have to do this bit because that's white.

(Pointed to a bit that was not yet coloured in, took out a green pen, made green marks above a red coloured patch.)

Kate: What are the green bits, John?

John: That's the bits you don't eat.

Julie: The leaves and the stem.

Piers: Yes, that's the leaves and the stem.

John: What is it ... the leaves and the stem.

(Took the yellow pen out of the pack.)

John: Now I need the little bits.

Piers: The seeds, John.

John: Yeah, the seeds.

(John carefully made small dots on the red patch eventually going through the paper.)

Kate: Try a different spot.

Julie: Careful, John, you're going through, just gently.

(John moved to another spot and made a little mark with the yellow pen.)

Piers: That's fine now.

John: There, that's a strawberry!

Kate: Thank you John and can I take this with me to show that you are okay about me coming into school?

John: Yes, ...Do you like strawberries?

Kate: Yes, I love them.

John: I picked them.

Kate: Did you pick them ... did you grow them in your garden?

Piers: No we went to the farm.

John: Yeah, we picked them at the farm. We had strawberry pie.

This episode illuminated many aspects of the mark-making process. Although persuasion by the adults and the nature of the situation seemed to have an impact, John showed great assertion in choosing to draw a strawberry. He seemed to prefer to represent an object rather than to follow the adult convention of writing his name. At this time he was just beginning to write his name independently. Was he choosing to draw something because there was less risk of 'getting it wrong', or did he feel that name writing was an activity best conducted at school? Either way his suggestion that the researcher should wait to see him write his name at school was a clever solution to the situation and allowed him to continue with his drawing plan.

The circumstances surrounding this episode illustrate the socio-cultural and emotional influences on children's thoughts and actions (Worthington and Carruthers 2003: 20). There are many possible reasons why John felt confident to draw a strawberry in this context:

- He felt supported and encouraged by the adults.
- He was able to use a red pen; red is his favourite colour.
- He liked strawberries.
- He had personal experience of picking strawberries and being involved in making and eating strawberry pie.
- He knew that you must be polite to visitors.
- He had personal positive experience of adults engaging with him at school.
- He liked adult attention.
- He wanted to respond positively to the request.

This was one of the first recorded observations of John making a representational drawing of an object. His use of marks in his drawing and his representations through his speech related to previous experience. The initial *enclosure* for the strawberry and the *infill* of colour, the yellow spots or *dabs* and the *connecting lines* or *trajectories* of green, all linked with previous learning through action (Athey 1990; Bruce 1997; Matthews 2003).

'Action, graphic and speech representations that convey dynamic space notions set within a three-dimensional world have their earlier equivalents at the sensorimotor stage' (Athey 1990: 160).

From action to mark making

In his book, *Drawing and Painting*, Matthews (2003: 43) describes how the earliest marks children make come from gestures that have been made repeatedly in infancy. The 'horizontal arc' and the 'vertical arc' come from the complex process of assimilating information into a *trajectory*. The natural swinging of the skeletal and muscular frame also plays a part in these early gestures.

Looking at John's Mark Making Portfolio we can follow the record of how he has explored *vertical* and *horizontal lines* and *dabs*. Between three and four years of age many of John's paintings also involved covering or '*enveloping*' the paper with paint. Nursery observations made around the same time record how John enjoyed being *enveloped* by balls in the ball pool. He also spent long periods of time *containing* sand and water in different containers.

Creating an impact

The perceptual feedback from the marks made using different movements encourages further exploration, just as the effects of repeatedly throwing, rolling or scattering objects are of interest to toddlers. To sustain the activity, children need to create an impact with their actions. The scribbling of a two-year-old will soon stop if the marks they are making fail to appear.

'The pleasure of being able to perceive predictable effects from known actions sustains the activity of mark and model making' (Athey 1990: 89).

Early marks are 'works of art'

These early compositions have an aesthetic value in their own right. John has explored the effects of moving his paint brush in different directions but he has also explored different combinations and positioning of colour and form. Matthews argues that the development of these early actions is not just as a result of attempts to master the manipulation of objects. He stresses that they form a basis for expression and communication with those around us and indeed are steeped in emotional value (Matthews 2003: 36).

As adults we are challenged to look at children's paintings and drawings in a new light. Instead of constantly trying to make 'adult sense' of what we see, we should appreciate the marks made from the child's perspective. Recognising what makes 'child's sense' enables adults to have insights into 'the child's current and developing understanding' (Worthington and Carruthers 2003: 12).

Matthews (2003: 13) argues strongly that the notion of 'visual realism' prejudices adults in the way that they respond to children's drawings and paintings. It also has a marked impact on creativity and individual expression through the way children's pictures are received.

Experienced environmental content precedes mark making

In her work during the Froebel Project, Athey (1990: 37) focused on observed behaviour patterns or schemas. She describes schemas as 'a pattern of repeatable behaviour into which experiences are assimilated and that are gradually co-ordinated. Co-ordinations lead to higher levels and more powerful schemas'.

Athey collated over 5,000 observations of twenty children, for a period of two years from the age of two, concentrating on the commonalities observed in their behaviour. In the course of the study she focused on their drawings and paintings and found that there was a correspondence between mark making and experienced environmental content (Athey 1990: 69).

Very young children experience *trajectories* (linear movements) with the developing control of their whole bodies or parts of their bodies before they draw a line. As babies learn to make gestures in both directions, they then begin to co-ordinate these movements into a 'push and pull' action. This is replicated later on in mark making (Matthews 2003: 22).

John's grids

The coordination of *horizontal* and *vertical trajectory* or *line* schemas leads to the formation of a *grid* schema (Athey 1990: 94). John had a particular interest in *grids* for a long time. The initial letter of his name, always a great source of interest due to its personal significance, is in itself formed by crossing a line.

Nursery observations recorded John's interest in his initial letter shape:

John three years, nine months and fourteen days

At lunchtime John had broccoli. He ate the 'trees' and left the stalks on his plate. He looked at the stalks and said 'That's my name' (it looked a bit like a J).

Right after lunch John got on a bicycle and asked me to attach two trailers. He rode around and kept looking behind at the trailers (he seemed interested in the shape he was making).

John's interest in *grid* formations is reflected in his first recorded representational drawing, 'a railway'.

John continued to repeat a *grid* like pattern in his games at school. He used a *grid* formation in a game of noughts and crosses.

John (five years today)

John: I'm going to draw some patterns now. That's an 'ex' where the treasure is.

Adult: Does that mark the spot?

John: Well it's just ... well, it's not going to be a spot... because it's going to be 'ex' with crosses. You have to do a circle or an 'ex'.

Adult: Oh I see ... what ... is that a game?

John: Yeah.

Adult: Can I play the game?

John: Yeah.

Adult: What do I have to do?

John: You have to ... you want to be a circle or the 'ex'?

Adult: Which one do I have to be?

John: You can ... you get... You're good at 'ex's', aren't you?

Adult: I'm quite good at 'ex's'.

John: 'You want to be the 'ex'. If you don't know how to do the circle, I'll make a circle here. That's doing a little circle like this.' (Points to the circle.)

Adult: Okay.

John: This circle shows you what you have to do.

Adult: Okay. So how about if I put an 'ex' in here (in the centre). What next?

John: You can do an 'ex' here or a circle ... you can do both if you want.

Adult: Can you? How do you play then ... what are the rules of this game?

John: You have to get four like this ... (draws three 'ex's' down the page) one, two, three ... and one more ... four (draws fourth 'ex').

Adult: And that means you win the game?

John: Yeah, you win the game.

As can be seen from the dialogue during this 'game', John was very aware of the challenges of mark making and needed to make sure that the adult was feeling confident enough to draw an X. He asked, 'You're good at those aren't you?' He also made sure that the adult had the support of his circle shape in case they had forgotten how to draw a circle. He had devised a key to communicate one of the rules of playing the game. He was demonstrating the actions of a considerate teacher.

John often showed through dialogue that he had an emotional concern or awareness during mark making, as seen during the 'drawing a strawberry episode'. This reinforced the view that there is a 'close relationship between cognition and affect' (Athey 1990: 97).

Seven days later John produced a huge display of letter shapes and drawings having been inspired at home by an alphabet book. His particular interest in the initial letter of his name 'J' was still very evident. He also pointed out all his 'favourite letters' which were I, H and J.

Observation

John (five years and nine days) brought the sheet of marks he had made at home in to school (Figure 7.1). He pointed to the initial letter of his name saying, 'That's my bestest letter'. He recognised his name upside down on the page and pointed out 'S' saying, 'That's Stephen's name'.

Among the letter symbols were drawings of grids which John called 'ladders'. When asked about them he reached for an action toy figure to climb the ladder saying, 'it's just to climb up ... to get these letters'. John pointed to the letters beyond the 'top' of the ladder.

Analysis and discussion

Here it seemed that John was working through his *grid* schema from his knowledge of ladders. He had an understanding of ladders from practical experience of their function (I step on here, I go up). He then demonstrated

Figure 7.1 John's alphabet sheet from home.

ladders symbolically – representing movement using the action figure and the drawing to represent a person moving up a ladder. He was able to articulate his understanding of the use of a ladder by suggesting that the man had climbed the ladder to 'reach the letters'.

Graphic schema: repeated patterns in use of lines and shapes

As we study children's drawings and listen to what they have to say about them, we see the same form or graphic schema being used to represent different content. We have already seen how John used a *grid* formation, which he has described at different times and in different drawings as a 'ladder' and a 'railway'.

Athey (1990) and Matthews (2003) have described the developmental sequence of graphic schemas. While the developmental order is not rigid, children tend to explore vertical and horizontal lines and arcs before they explore oblique and curved lines and circles. Co-ordinations of graphic schemas occur when lines are used together in different directions (*grid*) and when two structures are used repeatedly in a new form (*core with radial*).

Graphic Schemas
- horizontal arc
- vertical arc
- horizontal line
- vertical line
- semicircle
- circle
- oblique line.

Co-ordinations
- grid
- core with radial
- zigzag.

Graphic co-ordinations in space and position

As children develop their means of representation through mark making they begin to co-ordinate different graphic schemas to represent meaning through the spatial order and position of the marks. This can be illustrated by observations of children beginning to represent a person by drawing a face.

Bower (1977: 79) describes how as babies develop they respond to an increasingly sophisticated differentiation of the pattern of a face. They are progressively able to discriminate between the spatial order and shapes of facial features. This process is reflected in drawing development.

At four years and eleven months John began to represent people following a visit from his older cousin, Kieran. Kieran demonstrated representing people through different drawings during his visit. John was receptive to this and immediately began to explore the representation of a person in terms of drawing an *enclosure* within which he placed circles representing facial features. It seems that Kieran enabled John to move into his zone of proximal development by acting as a more capable peer as described by Vygotsky (1978: 86). 'Vygotsky's and Piaget's work show how important it is for younger children to see older children handling materials with confidence and pleasure' (Bruce 1997: 114). Within days John was drawing people at every opportunity. He was able to demonstrate his understanding of the spatial order of facial features and he began to explore the idea of the *connectedness* of the body by drawing legs at the bottom of the *enclosed* shape.

John represents people

John (four years, eleven months and twenty-six days) 'Do you know how to draw a smiley face? You have to have a head (draws *enclosure*) one big eye here and one big eye here (draws two smaller *enclosures* within large *enclosure* near the top) and a big smiley face (draws a curved line within the large *enclosure* at the bottom) and some legs and arms' (draws two lines extending from the bottom and two from the side of the *enclosure*).

John holds the picture up saying, 'There we go'.

Analysis and discussion

John seemed to have a set sequence to drawing the features he represented. In his next drawing however, on the same day, he demonstrated his secure knowledge about the reversibility of the process and chose to draw the features in a different order.

Observation

John drew an elongated *enclosure*. 'I'm doing a big smiley mouth first' (drew curved line within *enclosure* and then drew two lines extending from the bottom of the *enclosure*) He held up his picture to look at it (Figure 7.2).

'You know what I'm going to ... big arrows ... big arrows going to be the arms' (drew line at the edges of the *enclosure* and held the paper up again). 'There you go, what about think of that!'

Figure 7.2 'Tishy' by John at four years, eleven months and twenty-six days.

Analysis and discussion

After reflection, John went on to draw arms and related them to 'big arrows', a graphic form (directional lines) he was showing interest in during the same week. While he often stated that previous pictures represented different adults or peers, he proudly announced that this picture was of his sister. His elongated *enclosed* shape in his drawing was quite different from the more rounded shape of the *enclosure* representing other people. This could be coincidental but it could reflect John's perception that people, particularly toddlers, have different shapes to their bodies.

Observation

John built on his experience of representational drawings when four days later he decided to represent his cat.

John (five years today) drew two enclosures on paper 'That's the big teeth and that's my cat. And do you know what this is going to have to be ... (drew an elongated enclosure) ... my cat ... yeah ... that's my cat ... draw teeth'.

Adult: Where's the head?

John: This is the head there (pointing to the thin end on the left).

Adult: And these are ... (pointing to the enclosures within the elongated shape).

John: That's his eyes ... these are his eyes.

Adult: I see ... where's his mouth then?

John: Well, you see this little bit here ... (pointing to the thin end on the left) ... that's his mouth.

Adult: Where's his body?

John: Here (pointing to the bottom of the enclosure).

Adult: Has he got a tail, your cat?

John: This is his tail ... wait (draws a line extending from the enclosure to the right) there we go, that's his tail.

(John begins to draw lines extending from the thin end on the left.)

Adult: Oh, what are those?

John: Sharp teef.

Adult: Sharp teeth!

John: Cos cats need sharp teef.

Adult: Has he got sharp teeth?

John: Yeah (draws four lines extending from the bottom of the enclosure) ... and these are ... two legs here and two legs here ... there we go ... he needs two legs here and two legs there.

Adult: So how many legs has he got altogether?

John: There is just ... one, two, three, four (counting each line with his finger) ... cos he needs four legs, don't he.

Analysis and discussion

From the dialogue recorded during John's drawing of a cat, we can begin to understand the thought processes he went through as he made this representation. Although the questioning by the adult sought clarification of what he was doing, John (at five years) made his own representation. He included 'sharp teef', suggesting real experience of his cat and his knowledge of animals, as he reflected 'cos cats need sharp teef'.

He drew the legs in pairs 'two legs here and two legs here'. He made the point that the cat needs four legs, suggesting that John not only knew that there are two legs at the front and at the back, but that the cat needs this arrangement to be able to stand up. When asked how many legs there were, John counted them with his finger and commented 'cos he needs four legs, don't he'. John had a secure knowledge of 'four'.

This sequence contrasts with the observations of a child in Athey's study who represented four legs by a tally system. When asked to clarify how many legs there were, this child repeated the operation, resulting in his animal drawing having eight legs. In this instance, John seemed to use his understanding of four together with his experience of animals and previous knowledge of 'objects on legs' to influence his representation.

John appeared to have a moment of accommodation after drawing two central *enclosures* (which he said were the eyes) within the large *enclosure*. He seemed to begin to represent his cat through his now well-practised positional organisation of features in a 'smiley face' i.e. 'face to face view'. When asked 'where's the head?' he appeared to solve the problem of representing an animal that is different at one end from the other by choosing to distinguish between the head end which soon acquired 'sharp teeth' and later the 'tail end' where he drew a line for the tail i.e. showing the 'side view'.

Representing the front view and the side view simultaneously did not appear to create a problem for John. He was using his knowledge of his cat to represent what he knew about his cat. He was seeing what he drew in an abstract way. He was showing that his thinking was authentic and more flexible than conventions normally allow.

Case study: Caitlin, born 28 July 2000

Caitlin lives with her older brother Robert, who displays challenging behaviour and has additional needs. Robert has been diagnosed with Noonan's syndrome, a genetic disorder. Caitlin and Robert live with their mother, Anna.

Caitlin is a very engaging child. She is lively and sparky and she enthusiastically engages in new projects. She loved playing with water at nursery and her recorded schemas were *transporting*, *trajectory*, *containing* and *enveloping*. She really enjoyed dressing up and she would invariably clomp about in a pair of heeled dressing-up shoes. At the beginning of the project she enjoyed making marks on paper and using different coloured pens.

Curves and enclosed circles in emergent writing

Nursery records of the project children's graphic development show that circles and *enclosures* were apparent in early paintings and initial attempts to represent writing. Caitlin began to use curved lines and circular forms to represent writing.

In several of her paintings at school, Caitlin (four years, three months and thirteen days) chose to paint a curved line. The picture sequence (Figures 7.3–7.7) shows Caitlin painting; she had decided to paint 'a rainbow' (Figure 7.3). She covered the paper with different coloured paint following a curved line (Figure 7.4).

At nursery she loved to cover her hands with paint and it seemed she drew on these explorations when some paint fell on her hand and she began to finger paint. She covered the page reflecting her *envelopment* schema.

Figure 7.3 Caitlin's rainbow (I).

Figure 7.4 Caitlin's rainbow (II).

Figure 7.5 Caitlin's rainbow (III).

At the end of this sequence, she went on to paint a contrasting line across the curved lines (not shown in illustration). She seemed interested in this new possibility. On another occasion Caitlin (four years, three months and twenty-seven days) painted in white on a black background (Figure 7.6).

Caitlin drew curved lines in paint in contrasting colours. She turned her paper over to draw another pattern and folded the paper to compare the two, saying they were the same. She painted on the folded sheet saying 'c' as she painted another curved line.

She experimented with the paint eventually *enveloping* the whole paper and proceeded to fold the paper and wrap it up as 'a present for mum' (Figure 7.7).

She began to *envelop* the paper in paint, painting round the edge and then *filling in* all the gaps. She folded the paper. She said 'Don't tell my mum what this is ... it's a present ... cos it's her birthday today ... actually not today, it's just yesterday ... no, before yesterday ... no, after yesterday ... it's a present'. She wrapped it up in another paper.

Figure 7.6 Caitlin's monochrome rainbow.

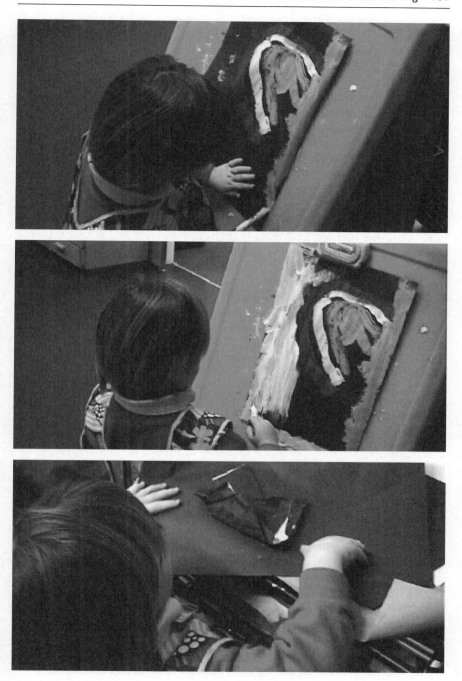

Figure 7.7 Caitlin's monochrome rainbow develops and changes.

Analysis and discussion

Caitlin's *envelopment* schema was explored through her painting. This is a familiar behaviour to many who are working with young children and corresponds to Cathy Nutbrown's observations of paintings creating a 'soggy hole' ... 'I've covered it up' (Nutbrown 1994: 45).

At three years and seven months, Caitlin was an accomplished mark-maker and spent time and concerted effort in attempting to form the letters of her name. She was interested in the curved line or arc. She formed the letter 'c' from an early age. When asked to copy the letter 'k' in a hand writing session at school, Caitlin (four years, three months and twenty-eight days) found the positioning of the oblique line very challenging. She was able to draw an oblique line on the paper but she found the positioning of the oblique lines in the letter 'k' difficult to replicate. Caitlin showed remarkable resilience when faced with this problem and tried many times without undue frustration or anger. She recognised how difficult this task was for her and observed, 'I'm trying to do it, but I can't'. She was then encouraged to write her name and received lots of praise and support from her teacher.

Athey details how research shows that 'at 6 weeks infants can see vertical and horizontal stripes better than oblique stripes (Leehey *et al.*, 1975, p 579)' (Athey 1990: 94). She also notes that children can copy vertical and horizontal lines before they can copy oblique lines. Many practitioners will recognise that four and five year old children often find drawing a tick or an arrow symbol to be particularly difficult.

Pedagogical conclusions and implications for practice

Understanding the developmental sequence in the use of lines and shapes has implications for learning and teaching or 'pedagogy'. We can help to extend learning by offering experiences that will engage children through their own interests and match their developmental concerns.

Recognising the schema that children are exploring gives us a very useful tool in identifying their interests and concerns, and enables us to provide worthwhile environmental content to extend their learning. Engaging in a respectful dialogue with children about the marks they make gives us an insight into their thinking and allows us to extend their thought.

The rich and individual ways in which children explore communicating through marks brings into question whole class teaching of graphic representation at this early age such as letter formation. Throughout many Foundation Stage 2 classes in the UK (four- and five-year-old children) the teaching of phonics and the teaching of letter formation is often conducted at the same time without regard for individual developmental concerns.

Looking at children's development in terms of their schemas can help us to think carefully about how and when we encourage children to 'have a go' at different challenges, following the child's lead. It is more beneficial for children and much more interesting for adults and children to work together on how representations are built up in relation to letters children have chosen to work on. There is a strong link between the letters children choose and their graphic schematic concerns of the time. Adults and children also benefit from recognising the significance the children attach to certain letters following their own concerns and interests.

Caitlin was fascinated at this time with curved lines. John was very motivated to draw the shapes of the letters that corresponded to his 'grid schema'. By supporting children's schematic interests, we build on what children can do, rather than steering them towards what they can not do.

If enabled to be free to do so in a supportive environment, children explore their own fascinations, develop mastery, and become experts in charge of their own learning. When they meet appreciation and affirmation by understanding adults and peers they experience a corresponding rise in self-esteem. Their efforts are valued. Their voice is heard. They engage in dialogue that extends their learning. They make connections and build on what they know.

If we are really going to maximise the learning potential for each child, we need to develop a community of learners, through involving parents as equal partners in their children's learning and listening to the child's voice (Whalley 2001: 22). Using schema theory enables us to respond to the children's interests and cognitive concerns. It helps us to provide a rich, positive and supportive learning environment.

Reflections and questions

We saw two children here smoothly making a transition into Foundation Stage 2.

- How often are the children's individual interests taken into account in what can be perceived as a more formal learning environment?
- How can children be encouraged to express their experiences in their own ways and be acknowledged for those expressions?
- If teachers took account of children's schematic interests, could they support the development of writing more effectively?

John's interests now

John is eleven years old (Figure 7.8). He remembers that he loved to play outside on the bikes and he also liked the trains. John enjoys art and computers, especially drawing on the computer. At the end of lessons he tries to sneak onto the games. John particularly enjoyed a gardening project at school. He was put in charge because he was 'more sensible at planting them'. They grew beans, carrots, spring onions, sunflowers and courgettes. John does not like work, tests or walking around the school by himself and gets a bit nervous about plays.

Figure 7.8 John now.

Caitlin's interests now (see p. 57).

Chapter 8

Transforming learning for children and their parents

Pam Cubey

This is an account of how parents/educators/researchers at Wilton Playcentre successfully combined their knowledge and understanding of schemas and Learning and Teaching Stories to support, extend and enrich their children's learning at home and in the Playcentre.

The first part of this chapter provides a short description of the New Zealand early childhood organisation known as Playcentre, and how it originated.

The second section was originally presented by me in a paper at the Pen Green Conference: *Understanding Young Children by Identifying their Schemas* at Corby on 24 June 2006. Much of the content was first published in *Transforming Learning at Wilton Playcentre* (van Wijk *et al.* 2006). It includes the writing of three parent/educators: Rebecca Bulman, Mary Craythorne and Michelle Wilson and the research associates: Linda Mitchell and myself.

The New Zealand Playcentre Movement

There is nothing quite like Playcentre. There are no other known organisations which integrate child and parent learning and train parents to become educators of their children, while at the same time expecting them to take collective responsibility for that education which involves establishing, organising and supervising play sessions as well as administering and maintaining the centre.

In Playcentres the basis of successful child education is the continuing education of the parents, focusing on children's learning and development.

Since its earliest days Playcentre has embraced these two distinct yet linked groups of learners, seeking their potential. 'Playcentre's strength lies in the combination of parents and children learning at the same time. If one considers that playcentres are providing merely, or even mainly, a service for children, then its essence is missed' (McDonald 1974: 160).

Dr Gwen Somerset, whose influence on Playcentre has been immense since its early beginnings until her death at the age of 93, described this dual emphasis on children's development and parent education as the ' "two wings" on the "butterfly" – they could not be detached, they had to work together for the "butterfly" to fly' (Stover 1998: 4).

How did an organisation like this come into being?

The first Playcentre was opened on 2 April, 1941, in Karori, the Wellington suburb in which I grew up and now live. That was 71 years ago in wartime, when there were many women struggling alone to rear their children whose fathers were overseas. It was pioneered by a group of highly educated, confident women with diverse skills, who were concerned for these mothers. There was already a favourable climate for such a venture in the educational community with which these progressive instigators were in touch.

A powerful influence was the New Educational Fellowship, founded in England, with branches in New Zealand. The Fellowship enabled Dr Susan Isaacs to travel to New Zealand in 1937 and give addresses in the four main cities. She impressed everybody with her emphasis on the importance of the early childhood years.

What about the philosophy and practice of Playcentre?

The philosophy and practice have developed from a potent mix of belief systems and social agendas, alongside its historic traditions and practices.

Playcentre was influenced by the thinking of overseas theorists such as Rousseau, Pestalozzi, Froebel, Piaget and such practitioners as Susan Isaacs, John Dewey and the McMillan sisters. In New Zealand, Gwen Somerset and Lex Grey 'embodied the tension between the "small" agenda of education and the "large" agenda of real social change' (Stover 1998: 55.).

Susan Isaacs' attitude towards children's play was one of respect for what the children are doing and what they might be learning. She valued new developments like water and messy and imaginative play within an environment of free play.

> Her beliefs had a considerable influence on the free choice philosophy of playcentre which was in sharp contrast to the prevailing attitude of the 1940s which saw a strict disciplinarian approach to child rearing and a belief that real education began only once children went to school
>
> (Stover 1998: 30–31)

A significant part of the pioneers' enduring legacy is the highly flexible, simple organisational structure that is characteristic of Playcentres even 71 years later.

Karori Playcentre was a community effort with a capable and confident committee. It was self-financing. It was self-organising. It was a simple transferable model using basic resources found in every New Zealand community.

In the postwar years Playcentre grew along with the baby boom. It spread throughout the country. The idea of organised early childhood education was introduced to communities where previously there had been none and it brought together diverse groups of people united by the desire to do the best for their children.

New centres opened where energetic parents came together. They operated in local halls and required no new buildings or protracted teacher training. Playcentres were able to reach farther into the countryside, making early learning accessible even for small groups of children. 'Gradually the realisation of the value of their own contribution snowballed among the parents and parent education prospered' (Densem and Chapman 2000: 41).

This effect is still one of the greatest strengths today.

The following quote from a Playcentre submission in 1973 is as relevant for Playcentres now in the twenty-first century:

> Our aim is to carry over into the home and family, ideas and attitudes demonstrated at playcentre. There is a reciprocal relationship between home and playcentre. As a result of work in playcentre the parent enriches family living; as a consequence of the experience of parenthood the parents enrich the preschool education of children
>
> (Densem and Chapman 2000: 58)

Ideally, through Playcentre, parents are able to find out how to use everyday experiences to enrich their children's lives and expand their ideas. The hope and expectation is that the learning experience for children and adults is not limited to the hours at the centre, but carries over into the home, family and community. So, parents can draw attention to, talk about, recall, anticipate and tie into the child's real life and understanding the new experiences and happenings.

'The impact of Playcentre's adult education on the lives of ordinary women is probably the longest and most enduring legacy of the movement' (Stover 1998: 16).

> Conceived in an optimistic tradition and raised in an optimistic time, Playcentre successfully demonstrated that parents can take responsibility for the education of their children. That idea is still a powerful one. The challenge for the 21st century is to hold onto that idea because, by their mere presence, playcentres validate parents who intuitively know that time spent with their children is valuable. Playcentre can show them how to make the most of that opportunity in an unforgettable way.
>
> (Stover 1998: 19)

Transforming learning for children and their parents (adapted from the Pen Green presentation)

It all started in 2002 when Wilton Playcentre was selected as one of six early childhood Centres of Innovation (COI) in New Zealand aimed at improving teaching and learning in early childhood education through action research.

A New Zealand government vision is that Centres of Innovation foster research and development and reflective practice in the early childhood education sector and reflect New Zealand's heritage of ingenuity and innovation. Sadly the present Government has discontinued the Centres of Innovation Project.

The idea is that 'centres capitalise on the experiences of those most likely to produce the best ideas through research – the people working in the ECE services. The teachers combine their skills with the complementary skills of researchers' to research their innovative practice' (Crown 2002: 15).

As a centre of innovation Wilton Playcentre was required to:

- provide effective approaches to improve early childhood learning and teaching based on *Te Whāriki*, New Zealand's early childhood curriculum;
- carry out action research to explore the effects of innovative approaches to learning and teaching and to develop resources to share with the early childhood sector; and
- share knowledge, understanding and models of good practice with colleagues and parents/whānau via a dissemination programme.

The findings in this paper are from a context framed by *Te Whāriki* in which the aspirations for children are that they will: 'grow up as competent and confident learners and communicators, healthy in mind, body and spirit, secure in their sense of belonging and in the knowledge that they make a valued contribution to society' (Ministry of Education 1996: 9).

These findings arose from one of our research questions:

> *In what ways does an understanding of schemas and Learning and Teaching Stories enable parent educators to support, extend and enrich children's learning at home and in the Playcentre?*

We found this question linked closely with another research area, that of parent engagement and sustaining a community of learners. We were looking, therefore, at both children's and parents' learning.

What are Learning and Teaching Stories?

A Learning Story is a documented account of a child's learning experience, (which often takes place across time and in different places). Several people often contribute to Learning Stories – typically educators, parents and children. The account is typically structured around five learning behaviours: taking an interest; being involved; persisting with difficulty; expressing a feeling or a point of view; and taking responsibility (Carr *et al.* 2000). These behaviours can be interpreted as learning dispositions.

At Wilton Playcentre we see dispositions as children's attitudes to learning, and to themselves as learners; whereas their inner-directed drives which we spot as schema interests lead children to learn by 'assimilating material, ideas and situations in the world into inner schemas and concepts' (Piaget 1953: 384). Chris Athey, drawing on Piaget, describes schemas as 'patterns of repeatable behaviours into which experiences are assimilated and that are gradually co-ordinated' (1990: 37).

A Teaching Story looks more particularly at the adult role in children's learning. The Teaching Stories are usually included within the Learning Story documentation. They record how adults are engaged in interactions with children, such as: guiding, scaffolding, co-construction, sustained conversations or making provision for enriching the play in order to foster positive dispositions to learning, and to facilitate children's learning theories. Wilton Playcentre's research found that children's schema interests often connect to children's working theories, and that adult-child interactions made children conscious of ideas connected to inner schema thoughts.

Why did we decide to bring our thinking about schemas and Learning Stories with their dispositions more closely together?

One of the reasons Wilton Playcentre was chosen as a Centre of Innovation was that parent/educators were already using schemas to help identify children's interests. I had introduced schemas to the Playcentre parents about four years previously in the form of professional development. Parents had embraced the theory enthusiastically and since then kept it alive in their practice. We were also familiar with Learning Stories, an assessment-research tool that focuses on dispositions, but we were not *really* thinking about schemas and Learning and Teaching Stories in combination.

We were influenced by Gill Poplur's recent master's thesis (2004), 'Early Childhood Teachers' Use of Schemas in Practice' in which she maintains that the interpretation of schemas and the development of dispositions do not need to be observed exclusively from one another. She proposed that New Zealand educators could better interpret children's thinking processes if initial observations of children's patterns of thinking were conducted inside Learning and Teaching Stories.

Poplur was a catalyst for us taking up the challenge to bring schemas and Learning and Teaching Stories together more effectively, to help us get a better grip on children's thinking and learning. The Centre of Innovation designation and Ministry of Education-funded resources made it possible to do the necessary research and development to learn more.

Another catalyst was parents realising, after analysing our baseline research data, that our processes of assessment, planning and evaluation were not very well connected.

We believe that schemas are helpful in illuminating children's *inner-directed* theories about patterns in the physical world while Learning Stories illuminate children's *dispositions* for learning as well as their content learning.

We need both if we are to reflect *Te Whāriki's* two overarching aims for children's learning, i.e. for them to develop working theories about their world along with positive learning dispositions.

We have come to see schemas as a theoretical nesting box for nurturing dispositions and planning for learning. When we provide for children's learning and support their explorations and passions, we create the conditions in which dispositions can develop and thrive.

How did we do this?

We became good spotters of schemas and describers of dispositions through adult learning processes: workshops and new members being mentored on the job by 'old hands'. Observation and documentation of Learning and Teaching Stories provided us with evidence for assessment, evaluation and planning. Over several months we worked at devising two new forms.

The first form is for assessment of children's learning by documenting Learning and Teaching Stories and identifying together schema interests and dispositions. It includes space for notes on what adults did — or could do — to take children's learning further. The second form is for evaluation and planning. This is carried out by the parent teams at the end of each Playcentre session. They use the completed assessment forms as a focus to aid them in their evaluation and forward planning.

The Wilton team has been mindful of Tina Bruce's advice (1997: 75–76), which said:

> One of the reasons why it would be unhelpful only to use schemas in looking at the development and learning of young children is that every theory has its range. It is important to look at the fitness of purpose of any theory and to draw on theories that complement each other and have some philosophical cohesion. This is very different from having an eclectic approach where bits and bobs of different theories are taken in isolated, unconnected ways. This leads to inconsistency, confusion and practice which constantly contradicts itself.

Our dual approach to exploring children's thinking and learning – and theoretical work we did in integrating the two approaches – changed our practice from eclecticism to coherence and connectedness.

Case studies

In exploring our research question, five parents carried out action research case studies of their own children. The Learning and Teaching Stories they collected over time at Playcentre, home and elsewhere, provided evidence of repeated patterns of behaviour as the children pursued their schema interests with energy, enjoyment and determination. It was a time of revelation and learning for both children and parents. We saw how the children's exploration of their schemas with assistance from adults and peers helped us to strengthen their dispositions to learning.

The parents were also looking for:

- continuity in schema-related exploration across Playcentre sessions;
- continuity in schema-related exploration between home and Playcentre;
- progression in their children's learning; and
- experiences that supported and extended that learning.

All five children demonstrated more than one schema interest, both before and during the study, and parents were able to identify and record progression of a dominant schema for each child. We found that these repeatable patterns showed progressions as children developed their working theories about their world.

The progression of schematic interests is as follows:
- from motor actions to
- symbolic representations (actions, mark making, visual art, and language) to
- functional dependency relationships to
- abstract thought.

(Athey 1990: 68)

Three of the case studies follow, mostly as told by the parents themselves.

Rosa

Rosa joined Playcentre when two weeks old, coming with her elder sister, Bella, and her mother, Rebecca.

At the beginning of her case study, when she was nearly two years old, she seemed to have five schema interests, the dominant one being trajectory, and particularly its vertical aspects (Figure 8.1).

Figure 8.1 Rosa then.

We saw progression in her thinking, first through *motor actions*. From an early age she enjoyed watching things that moved, especially balls, then later on she liked to dance with her sister, Bella, doing frequent spins and high leaps in a self-chosen, ballerina dress, and jumping. At the beginning of the case study she could jump down from a low chair unaided and jump high off the ground.

In Figure 8.2 she is playing with the hose and watching the water as it moves through the air.

Second, we noticed examples of *symbolic representation*, for example, drawing straight lines and using language to accompany her several motor actions. Words that were important to her were mainly verbs, and Rebecca has grouped them according to their schemas. One such trajectory word was 'whee' (swing), a first word. She would use it to refer to the swing itself but Rebecca was sure it originated from the action and her love of swinging high. Other verbs were 'run', 'dance', 'catch me' and 'climb'.

Rebecca says:

> 'Jump' is one of the most important words in her vocabulary. She has been using it since well before she had mastered the ability to do the action. Her first sentence was: 'I want to jump'. Our house is down 114 steps and if I would let her she would jump down each one but we have managed to reach a compromise and she jumps at the bottom of each flight of steps.

Figure 8.2 Rosa watching the moving water.

Figure 8.3 Rosa enjoyed jumping from an early age.

Rebecca used these schema-language links to further extend Rosa's vocabulary and increase her use of sentences. 'Rosa is more likely to learn words that are associated with her schemas because of her strong drive to do these things'.

'Climb' is another favourite word and an activity close to her heart. She is an avid climber and loves a climbing challenge.

And so we come to *functional dependency*.

'Rosa gets to the unattainable computer'

Rebecca is the photographer and the story teller.

> Here (Figure 8.4) you can see she has made her way to the computer after it had been put away to recharge the battery. She was most displeased as she had been looking at the photos with her father and me. Her strong drive to continue to play with it drove her to use her climbing skills. I did not see this happen as I was in the kitchen and then noticed that everything had gone too quiet.

But when Rebecca went to investigate she grabbed the camera and later wrote a Learning and Teaching Story.

Rebecca reconstructs what Rosa must have done:

> To do all this Rosa must have been able to put her knowledge of a number of things together: firstly, to get to the computer Rosa had to pull out the CD drawer, which she knew how to do as she does this about once a week to take the CDs out of their covers. She would have then climbed onto the chair on the right. She knew she could do this as it is at a height she feels comfortable about jumping from. Then it was a step onto the open drawer. At that point she could reach the computer which she opened by pushing the button to release the lid so she could resume where she left off. She must have observed us opening the computer and although I don't think she had actually done this before she knew how to open it.
>
> She was obviously chuffed with herself and gave me a great big smile until she realised I would take her down.
>
> The lack of adult input in this event has actually helped both Rosa and me. Rosa has been allowed to work through a complex set of problems to find a solution that achieves her goal and therefore has gained confidence in her own abilities to solve problems and be self-sufficient.
>
> I have seen how Rosa had developed her functional dependency reasoning to an extent I was not aware of. I would not have believed that she could do what she did without seeing her as she was photographed.

This story about schema learning indicates that Rosa, at age two years, seemed to be engaged in *abstract thought*. Her positive disposition toward

Figure 8.4 Rosa achieves her goal.

schema learning, and toward following adult models, jumped her into abstract thought.

The *dispositions* New Zealand early years educators look for in the Learning Story observations are:

- showing an interest
- being involved
- persisting with difficulty and uncertainty
- expressing an idea or feeling
- taking responsibility.

We think Rosa displayed all these dispositions in her own special way.

We asked the parents to give their thoughts about what they had gained from the case studies.

Rebecca said: 'Rosa has gained confidence in her physical abilities through having her attempts supported and encouraged. I think she has made fast progress because she has felt free to experiment knowing that she can rely on an adult assisting her if she needs it'.

Every attempt has been made to let Rosa continue in her play until she is 'finished'.[1] This has allowed her to practise as much as she wants to before trying something different.

> This study has made me a lot more aware of all the seemingly little or insignificant experiences or pieces of learning and their importance to the whole of the child's learning; each piece contributes to the whole. For example, one of the learning stories I did for Rosa was of her in her highchair with only a tumbler of water. She was putting her hand in the water and pulling it out, completely absorbed watching the drips fall down. In the scheme of things this exercise was essentially a time filler while she waited for food but she was getting a lot out of it which made it more than that. Children can get learning opportunities out of everything they choose to do and while the 'Golden Moments' are wonderful they have probably come about as a result of lots of little experiences being assimilated.

Matthew

Matthew has attended Wilton Playcentre since birth, with his mother, Michelle, and older brother, Jamie, and quite often with his dad, Charles. He was just over two years at the beginning of the case studies. In our data, he showed five schema interests, the dominant one being trajectory.

His case study explores how he is building on this trajectory interest in a range of ways including language, story, friendships, functional dependency and possibly abstract thought.

One of his happiest pastimes is throwing pumice or rocks into water in outdoor environments. He clearly gets a real sense of achievement out of it. As Matthew's mother reports:

> An example of Matthew's disposition of persistence in pursuing his trajectory schema was on a family holiday. He had been throwing rocks in a river. On the bush walk afterwards he picked up a large rock, struggling to carry it, resisting all suggestions that he leave it behind [until our return] to drop it off the bridge we had just passed or to try a smaller stone. Needless to say I ended up carrying the rock. He wanted to make a 'splash to the sky' and clearly knew he needed a big rock for a big splash.

Figure 8.5 Matthew at a favourite activity.

Matthew was really pleased with the splash into the biggest river, a 'splash to the sky'.

Matthew obviously was thinking through functional dependency. Because Charles and Michelle are well aware of his strong schema interest they go along with carrying his rocks as they appreciate how important they are to him.

At Playcentre, he sustains his interest in motion over a long time periods in exploring what will roll down pipes using a range of balls, creating his own continuity across Playcentre sessions, with the support and extension of Michelle, who is well in tune with his passion for trajectories. Matthew seems to be exploring the idea that if you place the ball in the pipe on a slope it will roll down and come out the other end (functional dependency). He is also finding out and categorising what will fit in the pipes and what will not.

Journeying might be thought of as a form of a trajectory schema although it could be an interest in transporting. However, Michelle thinks it is more of a trajectory interest given his longstanding fascinations with motion and currently with aeroplanes.

Figure 8.6 Matthew in the middle of a huge jump for his grandfather.

She said:

> This has become an important focus for Matthew in his dramatic play. He discovered this with his brother, Jamie, and Isabelle [our third case study child]. They went across the sea to see polar bears in Canada (some ideas from Jamie and some from Isabelle, such as doing up seat belts on the boat).

At a friend's house Matthew started a game of flying to Auckland to see the polar bears. Soon after at playcentre he suggested a game with another boy of flying to Auckland to see polar bears, doing up seat belts on the way.

His abstract stories have a lot of motion: He spontaneously told the following story, with no obvious prompts, which might be an example of abstract thought. It shows his developing ideas, using stories:

'Moggy, Clifford, Emily go in the aeroplane.
They get out, jump out on the grass
It crashed. They go in the aeroplane.
and a crocodile and a turtle ... and Mummy and Daddy,
Jamie, Mattie. We go in the aeroplane'.

Matthew used elements of this story, and the polar bear journey many times over the next few months. Trajectory language and imagery are foregrounded.

He enjoys open-ended questions to get both him and his friends thinking, and he picks up other children's ideas to incorporate with his own creative ideas in later stories, both at home and playcentre. As Matthew's parents we are able to make links to some of these ideas because of our knowledge of what happens at playcentre.

Matthew has always enjoyed trajectory motion. This fascination leads to much more than a simple interest in 'biffing' things. He enjoys using trajectory ideas and language, and with open-ended questions and ideas from other children, he is building a deeper understanding of his world. He is able to continue incorporating ideas from both home and playcentre to develop friendships, deeper and more abstract thought, and story-telling.

In the data, we saw him displaying such dispositions as *involvement*, *persisting with difficulty*, *expressing an idea* and *taking responsibility in joint attention episodes with others*.

In a very short space of time we have seen him involved in *energetic action*, *using symbolic representation*, *exploring functional dependency*, *recounting stories without physical prompts* and perhaps even *abstract thought*. He was but two and a half years old at the conclusion of the case study.

Michelle says:

One of the most rewarding parts for me is the chance to understand what is driving my own children. In our research I've really enjoyed looking at Matthew's schemas and all the ways they were helping him in his learning.

Isabelle

When the case study began Isabelle was two and three-quarter years old and had attended Playcentre since she was 15 months old with her mother, Mary, and baby brother, Aidan. She has shown us several schema interests and the dominant one is rotation.

Isabelle's interest in rotation showing elements of progression was first reflected in her *motor actions* dotted through observations in the Learning and Teaching Story records, at Playcentre and from observations at home written by Mary:

- wearing her 'circle dress' which flies into a circle when she twirls;
- drawing lots of circles and arcs, progressing to energetic circles and arcs with large rotational movements;
- using paint rollers for painting (Figure 8.7); and
- her fascination with stirring the pot (Figure 8.8).

Figure 8.7 Isabelle at home, rotating a roller to paint on a window

Figure 8.8 Isabelle was fascinated by rotation.

When Mary gave her the prompt, 'I've noticed that you are interested in things that go round and round', Isabelle replied, 'Like tyres'. This is an indication of her strong interest in vehicles with wheels, and in many books about them.

A clue to the intensity of her involvement is what has become known as her 'schema face': an open mouth, shaped like an 'O' and a frown of concentration, seen in the previous photos and in Figure 8.9.

Rotation is evident in her *symbolic representations*:

- mark making which imitates formal writing. Isabelle starts with small, fine, circular 'letters' and finishes with some bold, circular flourishes;
- a circular body and circular head are evident in her first drawing of a person (her friend's mother);
- role play of Samuel Whiskers and the *Roly Poly Pudding*, a favourite book, wrapping herself up in a rug and rolling on the floor; and
- rotating the embosser, and drawing circular marks on the paper that she passes through it.

Isabelle's dispositions show in her *intense interest* in things that rotate, accompanied by her *strong involvement and persistence* in her explorations as well as in *communicating her ideas through role play* and showing her parents the products of her work on the embosser.

Figure 8.9 Isabelle's 'schema face'.

Figure 8.10 Another manifestation of Isabelle's rotation schema.

Mary wrote:

A good example of how my knowledge of schemas has helped me is a group of observations at home and playcentre. At playcentre, Isabelle used an embosser to pass small pieces of paper through rollers by turning a handle. No stencil was used, so no impressions were made on the paper. Absorbed in this activity, she was very protective of the blank pieces of paper she produced. At one stage a boy, 'K', approached and picked up a blank piece of paper from the pile. Isabelle said 'No!' and stopped him with her hand. I gave Isabelle a standard line about sharing at playcentre. The issue was resolved when it was agreed that as there were two piles of paper, 'K' could have some from the other pile. Closer observation on my part revealed to me that the pile that was out-of-bounds to 'K' had already been rotated through the embosser. I noted on my [Learning and Teaching Story] observation sheet:

> I was wrong on reflection to ask her to share with 'K' the pieces of paper that had been rotated. This was as bad as letting a child draw on another's completed artwork!

The small pieces of paper were not blank to Isabelle. They seemed to represent an act of rotation she had performed on them, something of great interest to her. Forty three pieces of paper were taken home to show Daddy that evening, an indication of just how valued they were. Her father matched her enthusiasm with appreciative 'oohs' and 'aahs' as each apparently blank paper was produced. Two days later at home, she drew circles on each piece and showed each to both of us (one by one). She appeared to underline what the papers represented to her by her circular drawings on them. She repeated the activity at her next playcentre session.

Later, Mary wrote

The case study is a lovely snapshot of Isabelle's learning at these moments of time. On reflection, this was the peak of her interest in rotation. Her schema interests appear to be broadening and are more difficult to define and interpret as her learning becomes more sophisticated and complex. I have found that knowledge of her schema interests has helped me to reinterpret and deepen my knowledge of her behaviour.

Summing up

Although only three of the case studies are discussed here, all five have shown progression in the development of children's schema learning development.

All have demonstrated the sensorimotor action and symbolic representation and four of them have gone beyond that to abstract thought.

Rosa, in her desire to reach the computer, leads us to think that she has made the connection of 'If I do this, then that will happen' even though she is not yet able to verbalise this functional dependency.

Matthew was also working on functional dependency when he knew that by throwing a big rock into the river he would make a 'splash up to the sky'.

Although former studies have found that abstract thought is hard to identify in children of this age, we wonder if Matthew's story of Moggy, Clifford and Emily going up in the aeroplane may be such an example.

Hand in hand with the children's determination to explore their schemas we have seen their dispositions of curiosity, trust, playfulness, being involved, engaging with challenge, perseverance (sometimes in the face of difficulty), expressing an idea or feeling (verbally or non-verbally), and taking some responsibility for their own actions in joint attention episodes with others.

Rosa and Matthew began at Playcentre when they were babies and from a very early age developed the sense of well-being and belonging in what has become their second home. They also gained from being accompanied by their parents and their older siblings.

At the commencement of the case studies they knew the environment well and where they could access the materials and equipment that matched their schema fascinations. Their dispositions of independently finding something of interest and being involved were already firmly established.

Each of the five case-study children also provided evidence of continuity of learning. The children's explorations of their schemas continued across Playcentre sessions and between Playcentre and home and other places. Older siblings and friends were seen to enter into the play and offer new ideas and challenges thus stimulating further continuity.

A key factor which has supported continuity in exploring a pattern of thought – a theory – is the adults' knowledge and understanding of children's schemas. Thus, parent/educators are able to communicate across the different learning contexts what their children's driving interests are and help to enrich and extend them.

Throughout the studies, parents engaged with their children, following their lead, showing a genuine interest and appreciation of their children's learning and providing extra content and possibilities for extension.

Parents writing case studies speak with delight and an air of excitement at the insights and understanding they have gained of their children's thinking and 'coming to know'.

In conclusion

Through the action research cycles within the Centre of Innovation project, parent educators and their research associates at Wilton Playcentre successfully brought together two different (and in some views, oppositional) theoretical frames that until then had been used in parallel. As educators, our teaching and learning approaches drew strongly on both schema learning theory, which emphasises children's inner drives and derives from developmental psychology, and learning dispositions, which are based on sociocultural theory. We saw schema interests afford lots of opportunities for social learning.

In recent times, developmental psychology has been criticised for over-emphasising biologically determined stages of development rather than experience. Our findings, however, are that we were able to use the two theoretical approaches to complement each other. Together they helped us have greater depth of insight into children's learning progressions and how we might strengthen them. Our knowledge of schemas and observations of children at home and at Playcentre enabled us to identify children's schema interests. These schema interests rang true for us as we observed how children were driven to explore their schemas across different areas of play and in different contexts.

Our findings suggest that rather than the Playcentre experience helping children to 'find an interest' (a learning disposition), children come to the Playcentre with existing schema interests. Schema interests and dispositions seem to go hand in hand: children displaying a strong schema showed a drive to know and experiment, and this was associated with dispositions, such as showing an interest, being involved, persisting, expressing an idea or feeling and taking some responsibility for their own actions in focused attention with others. We argue that schemas may provide a basis for dispositions to flourish when schema interests are supported and extended.

Understanding schemas helped us make sense of play that we may not have otherwise tolerated. Noticing interests was a first step in being able to recognise and respond to them. We were helped in doing this by being prepared to 'see the unexpected' and not to prejudge levels of thinking because of a child's age. Rosa's computer story, suggests Rosa (two and a bit years) was able to use complex functional dependency ideas at a very young age, before we might have thought she could.

The Playcentre philosophy provided a basis for our sociocultural view of learning. We viewed adults and children as active joint participants in learning, and found ways to extend this participation and learning.

Prout (2005: 69) has suggested the need to 'include the excluded middle of dichotomies that have been made oppositional'. It may be that bringing together schemas and dispositions makes a contribution to finding a 'middle' between developmental psychology and sociocultural theory.

Our Centre of Innovation research project has worked well for us at Wilton Playcentre and we hope that it will help other early childhood centres too.

Reflections and questions

- How might such continuity between home and setting support young children's learning?
- How is language reflected in young children's explorations of schemas? How might adults capitalise on those connections between actions and language?
- Is it always helpful to allow young children to move on in their own time?

Acknowledgement

Funding for this research project was provided by the New Zealand Ministry of Education.

The children's interests now

Rosa

As we discussed, Rosa is very much into transforming at the moment (Figure 8.11). Most nights she is some sort of animal – often a cat or a dog but last night she was a seal.

She moves around like the animal and makes animal sounds. The trajectory schema is still there and is expressed in her love of bike-riding in particular, speed is very important.

Rebecca (mother)

Figure 8.11 A photo of Rosa, chosen by herself, aged six years, three months.

Matthew

Matthew is seven years old now (Figure 8.12) and retains his interest in balls and movement. He is very physical and loves sports as well as all things outdoors.

He is also a very good reader particularly enjoying books with plenty of action. It's great to watch his enthusiasm for learning – whales and dolphins was his favourite topic last year, especially the diving of the sperm whale!

Michelle (mother)

Figure 8.12 Matthew now.

Isabelle

Isabelle is seven years five months in the photo (Figure 8.13).

It's hard to spot schemas with her nowadays. She still gets that schema face at times of deep concentration and interest sometimes unexpectedly if she is doing art, pouring cereal, wiping suncream into her skin, but I haven't detected a clear pattern for when it occurs. (Then again I haven't been observing in an analytical way either!)

Figure 8.13 Isabelle now.

She is interested in ballet and dance and likes to read. She likes to do art (drawing, painting) and crafty things.

I said to her: You used to like things that went round. She replied Yes, and I like to sit in things that go round. On further questioning, she meant things that rotate in playgrounds. Again, I said You also liked layers. She said Yes, I like to put layers on my sandwiches, like tomato, lettuce, cheese.

I don't think any particular conclusions can be drawn from this, but it would be interesting to take the time to explore.

Mary (mother)

Chapter 9

Drawing our learning together from the case studies

Cath Arnold

Introduction

The evidence gathered over time by workers and parents and presented in this book has helped us to illuminate some aspects of learning. In this final chapter, I intend to reflect on some important concepts raised by Chris Athey in Chapter 1 as well as addressing some common queries about schemas.

Constructivism

As early childhood educators, we are interested in how children learn. Like Piaget and, subsequently Chris Athey, we believe that children construct their own understanding of the world through experimenting and through their own first-hand experiences (Piaget 1971; Athey 1990). Within constructivist theory, learners are actively engaged. Those actions can be physical, intellectual and/or emotional. In order to learn, we make connections between what we know already and something new. We can trace some of those processes in young children's explorations. The concept of 'involvement' helps us to recognise when learning is taking place (Laevers 1997). When children are deeply involved, often their explorations are schematic. According to Athey, 'Within a constructivist pedagogy, the teacher seriously considers what the child brings to the learning situation, as well as what he or she wishes to transmit' (1990: 31).

We become engaged in learning about what children are exploring, rather than taking our lead from a curriculum document. However good that document is, it can never replace directly observing learners in action. We begin with children and make links with the curriculum. Proulx explains

> Constructivists are interested in the individual's construal of knowledge, that is, how a person comes to learn ... all knowledge is subjective and dependent on the learner. Instead of talking about an internal representation that reflects the external world, constructivism describes personal knowing in terms of fitting to and compatibility with the experiential world (2006: 2).

Rather than thinking about knowledge as something in the world to acquire or accumulate, constructivists see knowledge 'as an ever-evolving process' (Proulx 2006: 5). We can see this clearly, when young children express their current 'working theory' about something.

I remember a conversation with Alex, aged three:

Alex: Do you know Martin?
Cath: No, I don't know Martin.
Alex: Say 'Martin'
Cath: Martin.
Alex: You know Martin now.

Even this short conversation told me quite a lot about Alex's understanding of how we get to know people or maybe he meant 'know about people'. His working theory was that if you say their name, then you must know them (or maybe know about them).

As adults working with young children, our role is not passive but 'it is the learning process of the learner that becomes the entering door' (Proulx 2006: 11). Detecting schemas is exciting work, because even though the patterns are universal, we never quite know how or when or for how long children's schematic interests will last. There is, of course, a developmental aspect to the emergence of schemas but it seems so complex and diverse that predicting a pattern or set of patterns in advance can seem almost impossible. That does not stop us from trying.

Content and form

The 'content' of children's play is what they are playing with and the 'form' what they are 'doing' with what they are playing with. For example, if, as Chris Athey points out, we notice a child's interest in 'clocks' (content), we might offer a range of 'timepieces' for them to explore. However, when we realise that the child is also interested in what the clock does (the underlying 'form' or schema is *rotation*), this opens up endless possibilities for extending the learning across content that can be rotated, everything from whisks to globes to the solar system.

The evidence from these case studies clearly shows that children notice and are interested in 'form' as well as 'content'. While 'content' can vary over time and space, 'form' is invariant. Similar 'form' can be recognised right across areas of learning. 'Form' can manifest itself in actions and marks (configurations). For example, when Jack was interested in the 'form' of *intersections* and *grids* he recognised similarities across the 'content' of railway lines, a cross etc. He was also interested in how that 'form' was made (the actions needed to make materials resemble that 'form').

Co-ordinations

Progress can be traced when children co-ordinate the different schemas. Robert explored *trajectory*, *enveloping* and *going through a boundary* and subsequently became interested in growing a sunflower. This involved *enveloping* the seed in soil, watering and watching for the seed to sprout and come *through* to the surface of the soil. Then he spent many weeks measuring the height of his sunflower (*vertical line* linked to the *up/down trajectory* movement). Exploring the schemas helped Robert to understand the concept of growing a flower from seed, something that could be co-ordinated and generalised to other plants and into his thinking about how plants grow.

As well as co-ordinating several schemas in their thinking, children co-ordinate schemas in their actions (remember learning to drive or ski?) Caitlin co-ordinated her actions in order to release soap from a soap dispenser into a container. In this instance, she had to use two hands and simultaneously push a button (*horizontal trajectory*) while holding a receptacle capable of *containing* the soap as it came *through* from the dispenser. We become adept through practice and eventually our brains make our sets of actions automatic so that we do not have to consciously concentrate on co-ordinating practised sets of actions.

Assimilation and accommodation

We saw each of the study children 'assimilate' new content into their current schemas. For example, Steffi played with flour, cornflour, slime, shaving foam, sand and soil and experienced the different properties and what happened when materials were combined.

Occasionally, we noticed that a child had to 'accommodate' their actions or thinking when something unexpected happened. Steffi was surprised that some baby animals have completely different names from their parents. However, she was able to 'accommodate' this new piece of learning. Her 'working theory' up to that point and the generalisation that she was making, was that adults and babies from the same species have similar names. Ethan discovered that engines would not connect to the back of the carriages but he 'accommodated' his actions and then spent time moving his train behind the spare engine, thus propelling it around the track.

Piaget explained this sort of surprise by talking about 'equilibration' and 'disequilibration'. Other researchers have used words like 'disruptions in thinking', 'perturbation' and 'cognitive jar'. Whatever language we use to describe this process, it clearly describes what happens when something does not fit with our expectations and we have opportunities for new learning and understanding.

Repeated patterns or obsessions

Whenever educators and/or parents discuss the concept of schemas, the issue of what is 'obsessive' and what is 'normal' repetitive behaviour arises. We understand from the literature on children who are on the autistic spectrum, and from our observations, that children with autistic tendencies do indeed use schemas to learn. Some individual children also use repeated behaviours or actions for security. The issue may be that occasionally a child seems not to be developing any new behaviours or that adaptation is very slight and subtle (Shaw 2010). Jordan and Powell (1995: 49) point out that: 'Obsessions should not be "stamped out" but extended creatively, where possible, and others replaced with behaviour that serves the same purpose for the child'.

We believe that children are constructing their understanding of the world through repeating patterns. Our aim, therefore, with any child, is to extend their repertoire through offering content and experiences (Arnold 2010).

Gender differences

Another common query from educators and parents is whether there are differences in the dominant schemas explored by boys and girls. Although there are indications from small numbers of individual children, that boys may be more focused on *trajectory* and *connecting* behaviours and girls may have a stronger focus on *containing* and *transporting*, this finding is not conclusive (Arnold 2010: 151). As we have seen in the case studies presented in this book, children explore clusters of schemas usually across the range of common schemas. It would not seem helpful to limit experiences for boys or girls. Occasionally, children may be attracted by different 'content', for example, Lee was interested in going off with the boys and dressing up as a fireman and Caitlin was more interested in continuing their game of babies.

How young children experience and express their current cognitive concerns

Up until recently, we have followed Piaget and Athey in talking about 'levels' at which schemas are explored. However, we think that we need a new way to express this idea as the development is not strictly hierarchical. When talking about 'levels', we infer a kind of simple hierarchical structure. The development of understanding and knowledge is more complex than this model would suggest. As human beings, we gather different information from objects, other people and ourselves (Figure 9.1).

We gain different information and can also express different ideas in these ways. For example, if you watch a professional golfer lining up a long putt, s/he uses all of these ways of considering the putt. A golfer often 'walks the distance' to feel it, does lots of looking and visualising a 'symbolic' line

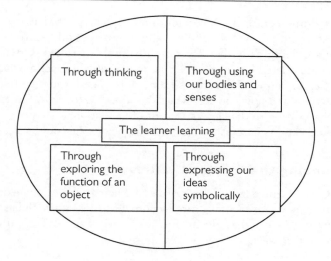

Figure 9.1 How the learner learns.

between the ball and the hole. S/he thinks about it and also practises the functional aspects i.e. the ball going into the hole is 'functionally dependent' on the golfer hitting it in the right direction at the right speed. So s/he practises the movement of the putter and in the direction of desired travel. We visit and revisit these different ways of experiencing and expressing our ideas. This does not mean that a newborn has this whole repertoire to use. We are used to recognising thinking when people express their thoughts in words but we do not really know when young children start to think and plan. We think that it is connected to language but we cannot be absolutely sure. We sometimes see young children concentrate and then carry out a set of actions. We say that we can almost 'see them thinking'. So we are open to new ways of expressing these ideas and also recognise that differentiating between these different ways of learning and expressing is useful.

The role of the adult

The evidence so far suggests that the adult can play a role, mostly in noticing and articulating a child's actions. Research on the brain suggests that a word can act as a 'pivot' in bringing together different experiences of a common pattern. Traditionally, early childhood educators would ask questions, for example, 'What colour is it?' or 'How many are there?' with learning concerned with being able to label the different colours or count to ten or more. This type of questioning does not take into account the child's concern but focuses on the adult's idea of learning outcomes. Knowledge of children's schematic concerns suggests that when young children are exploring schemas (patterns) they are building concepts. One definition of a schema is that it is a partial concept (Athey 2005). Accompanying language helps children to be aware of what they are doing and what the related concept is called. Often children themselves use related language and this, too, needs some acknowledgement. For example, Steffi used the words 'slidey', 'slippy' and 'squashy' to articulate both her actions and how clay felt when she added water to it. She recognised what was happening to the clay as a result of her actions.

Rosa could express her wish to 'jump' long before she could actually jump.

Underpinning theories and values

The Pen Green Centre for Under Fives and Their Families opened in 1983. Staff and parents wrote a Curriculum Document in 1986, which has stood the test of time. Within that document, what we wanted for children was articulated in this way:

- Children should feel strong.
- Children should feel able to challenge.
- Children should be able to question.
- Children should be able to choose.

We wanted to foster children's resilience. We also wanted children to be able to follow their individual interests. Schema theory has made it possible for us to understand specifically what the children are investigating and learning and to support their explorations. Back in 1986, we might have been in danger of taking a laissez-faire approach and contributing little to assist children's development of concepts. However, by noticing and articulating children's actions and by providing other resources and stories to 'feed' their cognitive concerns, we think we have found a useful role that does help contribute to children's development. The more that we can notice what children are giving attention to, the better we can support their explorations.

The other strand running through this book is the strong role parents play in understanding and articulating their children's learning. We would like to finish by reminding ourselves and you, as a reader, of what Chris Athey said in 1990:

> Nothing gets under a parent's skin more quickly and more permanently than the illumination of his or her own child's behaviour. The effect of participation can be profound.

(p. 66)

Bibliography and Reference List

Arnold, C. (1990) 'Children Who Play Together Have Similar Schemas' unpublished project submitted as part of a Certificate in Post Qualifying Studies, Peterborough Regional College.

Arnold, C. (1999) *Child Development and Learning 2-5 years: Georgia's Story*, London: Paul Chapman.

Arnold, C. (2003) *Observing Harry: Child Development and Learning 0-5 years*, Maidenhead: Open University Press.

Arnold, C. (2010) *Understanding Schemas and Emotion in Early Childhood*, London: Sage.

Athey, C. (1990) *Extending Thought in Young Children: A Parent-Teacher Partnership*, London, Paul Chapman.

Athey, C. (2003–2006) personal communications.

Athey, C. (2005) Personal Communication 10 November 2005 as an Expert Witness.

Athey, C. (2007) *Extending Thought in Young Children*, 2nd edition, London: Paul Chapman.

Barnes, P. (ed.) (1995) *Personal, Social and Emotional Development of Children*, Oxford: Blackwell.

Bion, W. (1962) *Learning from Experience*, London: Heinemann.

Bower, T.G.R. (1974) *Development in Infancy*, San Francisco: W.H. Freeman.

Bower, T.G.R. (1977) *A Primer of Infant Development*, San Francisco, W.H. Freeman.

Bowlby, J. (1969) *Attachment and Loss Volume 1: Attachment*, New York: Basic Books.

Bowlby, J. (1991) *Attachment and Loss Volume 2: Separation, Anxiety and Anger*, London: Penguin Books.

Bruce, T. (1997) *Early Childhood Education*, London: Hodder & Stoughton.

Capra, F. (1982) *The Turning Point: Science, Society and the Rising Culture*, New York: Flamingo/Fontana.

Carr, M., May, H., Cubey, P., Hatherly, A. and Macartney, B. (2000) *Learning and Teaching Stories: Action Research on Evaluation in Early Childhood Education*, Wellington: New Zealand Council for Educational Research.

Concise Oxford English Dictionary (1990) Oxford: Oxford University Press.

Corsaro, W. (2003) *We're Friends Right?* Washington DC: Joseph Henry Press.

Dahlberg, G., Moss, P. and Pence, A. (1999) *Beyond Quality in Early Childhood Education and Care: Postmodern Perspectives*, London: RoutledgeFalmer.

Damon, W. (1977) *The Social World of the Child*, San Francisco: Jossey Bass.

Das Gupta, P. and Richardson, K. (1995) 'Theories of Cognitive Development', in V. Lee and P. Das Gupta (eds) *Children's Cognitive and Language Development*, Oxford: Blackwell Publishers.

Davies M. (2003) *Movement and Dance in Early Childhood*, 2nd edition, London: Paul Chapman Publishing Ltd.

Dennison, M. and McGinn, M. (2004) 'At Home', *Nursery World*, 21 October, online, available at: www.nurseryworld.co.uk/news/723374/home/?DCMP=ILC-SEARCH.

Densem, A. and Chapman, B. (2000) *Learning Together, the Playcentre Way*, Auckland: Playcentre Publications.

Dewey, J. (1938 [1976]) *Experience and Education*, London: Collier Books.

Dunn, J. (1993) *Young Children's Close Relationships*, London, Sage Publications.

Faulkner, D. (1995) 'Play, Self and the Social World' in P. Barnes (ed) *Personal, Social and Emotional Development of Children*, Oxford: Blackwell.

Gopnik, A.M., Meltzoff, A.N. and Kuhl, P.K. (1999) *Scientist in the Crib: Minds, Brains and How Children Learn*, New York: William Morrow and Company.

Gussin Paley, V. (2004) *A Child's Work*, London: University of Chicago Press.

Hartup, W.W. (1983) 'Peer Relations' in P.H. Mussen (ed) *Handbook of Child Psychology: Vol 4, Socialization, Personality and Social Development*, New York: John Wiley, pp. 103–196.

Hunt, J.M. (1961) *Intelligence and Experience*, New York: Ronald Press

Isaacs, S. (1933) *Social Development in Young Children*, London: George Routledge and Sons.

Jordan, B. and Henderson, A. (1995) 'Interaction Analysis: Foundations and Practice', *Journal of the Learning Sciences*, 4(1): 39–103.

Jordan, R. and Powell, S. (1995) *Understanding and Teaching Children with Autism*, New York: Wiley.

Kant, I. (1781/1787 [1963]) *Immanuel Kant's Critique of Pure Reason*, trans. Norman Kemp Smith, London: Macmillan Co. Ltd.

Laevers, F. (1997) *A Process-Oriented Child Follow-up System for Young Children*, Leuven: Centre for Experiential Education.

Lee, V. and Das Gupta, P. (eds) *Children's Cognitive and Language Development*, Oxford: Blackwell.

Leehey, S.C., Moskowitz-Cook, A., Brill, S. and Held, R. (1975) 'Orientational anistropy in infant vision', *Science*, 190(4217): 900–902.

Maclellan, E. (1997) 'The Importance of Counting', in I. Thompson (ed.) *Teaching and Learning Early Numbers*, Buckingham: Open University Press.

Matthews, J. (2003) *Drawing and Painting: Children and Visual Representation*, London: Paul Chapman Publishing.

McDonald, G. (1974) 'Educational Innovation: The Case of the New Zealand Playcentre', *Journal of Educational Studies*, 9(2): 153–165.

McGinn, M. (2003) Researcher's Meeting at Pen Green Centre, Corby, Northants.

Meade, A. and Cubey, P. (1995) *Thinking Children: Learning about Schemas*, New Zealand Council for Educational Research and Institute for Early Childhood Studies, Wellington College of Education/Victoria University of Wellington.

Ministry of Education.Nelson, K. (1988) 'Where Do Taxonomic Categories Come From?', *Human Development*, 31(1): 3–10.

Nutbrown, C. (1994) *Threads of Thinking*, London: Paul Chapman Publishing. Oers, B. Van (1997) 'The narrative nature of young children's iconic representations: some evidence and implications', *International Journal of Early Years Education*, 5(3); 237–245

Pen Green Research Base (2004) *Growing Together Training Resources*, Corby, Northants.

Piaget, J. (1951 [1962]) *Play, Dreams and Imitation in Childhood*, London: William Heinemann Ltd.

Piaget, J. (1953) *The Origin of Intelligence in the Child*, London: Routledge and Kegan Paul.

Piaget (1971) *Structuralism*, London: Routledge and Kegan Paul.

Piaget, J. (1980) *Six Psychological Studies*, Brighton: Harvester Press.

Piaget, J. (2001) *The Psychology of Intelligence*, London: Routledge.

Piaget, J. and Inhelder, B. (1956) *The Child's Conception of Space*, London: Routledge & Kegan Paul.

Poplur, G. (2004) 'Early Childhood Teachers' Use of Schemas in Practice', unpublished MEd thesis, University of Auckland, Auckland.

Proulx, J. (2006) 'Constructivism: A Re-equilibration and Clarification of the Concepts, and Some Potential Implications for Teaching and Pedagogy', *Radical Pedagogy*, 8(1): 1–20.

Prout, A. (2005) *The Future of Childhood*, London/New York: RoutledgeFalmer.

Raban, B., Ure, C. and Waniganayake, M. (2003) 'Acknowledging the Virtue of Complexity in Measuring Quality', *Early Years*, 23(1): 67–77.

Shaw, J. (1991) 'An Investigation of Parents' Conceptual Development in the Context of a Dialogue with a Community Teacher', PhD thesis, University of Newcastle

Shaw, J. (2010) Conference Talk, 23 January, Pen Green Research Base, Corby, Northants.

Soale, V. (2004) 'I'm not Harry Potter am I? What's Going on Inside John's Head?' MA thesis, London Metropolitan University

Spencer Pulaski, M.A. (1971) *Understanding Piaget: An Introduction to Children's Cognitive Development*, New York: Harper and Row Publishers.

Stern, D. (2005) Research Seminar, 11 November, Pen Green Research Base, Corby, Northants

Stover, S. (1998) *Good Clean Fun: The New Zealand Movement*, Auckland: Playcentre Publications.

Sullivan, H.S. (1953) *The Interpersonal Theory of Psychiatry*, New York: Norton.

Tait, C. (2004) 'Chuffedness', presentation at the European Early Childhood Educational Research Association Conference, Malta.

Te Whäriki: He Whäriki Matauranga mo nga Mokopuna O Aotearoa, Early Childhood Curriculum, Wellington: Learning Media.

van Wijk, N., Simmonds, A., Cubey, P. and Mitchell, L. with Bulman, R., Wilson, M. and Wilton Playcentre members (2006) *Transforming Learning at Wilton Playcentre*, New Zealand Council for Educational Research.

Vygotsky, L. (1978) *Mind in Society*, Cambridge, MA: Harvard University Press.

Vygotsky, L. (1986) *Thought and Language*, Cambridge, MA: MIT Press.

Whalley, M. (2001) *Involving Parents in their Children's Learning*, London: Paul Chapman Publishing.

Whalley, M. and Arnold, C. (1997) *Effective Pedagogic Strategies*: *TTA Summary of Research Findings*, London: Teacher Training Agency.

Winnicott, D.W. (1965) 'The Theory of the Parent-Infant Relationship (1960)' in his *The Maturational Processes and the Facilitating Environment*, London: Hogarth Press.

Worthington, M. and Carruthers, E. (2003) *Children's Mathematics Making Marks; Making Meaning*, London: Paul Chapman Publishing.

Wylie, C. and Hipkins, R. (2006) *Growing Independence: Competent Children at 14*, Wellington: Ministry of Education, online, available at: www.nzcer.org.nz or www.minedu.govt.nz.

Index